D0451429

BEARS
in the Backyard

BEARS
in the Backyard

Big Animals, Sprawling Suburbs,
and the New Urban Jungle

Edward R. Ricciuti

THE COUNTRYMAN PRESS
WOODSTOCK, VERMONT

Book design and composition by Eugenie S. Delaney

Published by The Countryman Press, P.O. Box 748, Woodstock, VT 05091

Distributed by W. W. Norton & Company, Inc., 500 Fifth Avenue, New York, NY 10110

Printed in the United States of America

Library of Congress Cataloging-in-Publication Data are available.

Bears in the Backyard
978-1-58157-217-9

10 9 8 7 6 5 4 3 2 1

Photo credits. *pages 2–3:* © Den Donohue/**Shutterstock**.com; *pages* © Darren J. Bradley/Shutterstock.c *pages 6–7:* © Julie Lubick/Shutters com; *page 9:* xpixel/ Shutterstock.c *page 15:* Matt Knoth/Shutterstock. *page 20:* © creativex/Shutterstock. *page 38:* © Volodymyr Burdiak/Sh terstock.com; *page 54:* © David Sh bone/Wikimedia Commons; *page 5* Tony Campbell/Shutterstock.com; *62:* © Sarah Cheriton-Jones/Shutte com; *page 69:* © Neil Burton/Shut stock.com; *page 72:* © Matt Knoth Shutterstock.com; *page 96:* © Critt Shutterstock.com; *page 116:* © To Reichner/Shutterstock.com; *page* © Maria Dryfhout/Shutterstock.co *page 146:* © Juan Gracia/Shutters com; *page 152:* © Raffaella Calzon Shutterstock.com; *page 161:* © Su Flashman/Shutterstock.com; *page* © Heiko Kiera/Shutterstock.com; *168:* © Firman Wahyudin/Shutters com; *page 177:* © Irina oxilixo Da Shutterstock.com; *page 186:* © Ja Mintzer/Shutterstock.com; *page 2* Becky Sheridan/Shutterstock.com;

To Annie and Rick
For their love and support

CONTENTS

INTRODUCTION

The intrinsic creepiness of Alfred Hitchcock's 1963 film *The Birds* arises from the way it leaves us hanging, with what one reviewer called the "lack of a comforting explanation." The iffy ending of the film suggests that the full story has yet to unfold, and when it does, it will not be pleasant. By never providing a rationale for why the birds have begun to savage humans, the film, which borrows from a story of the same name by Daphne du Maurier, toys with the same primal fears that can make us feel edgy in the dark for no apparent reason.

The story's motif, birds gone wild, did not originate with du Maurier. *The Birds* is also the title of a 1936 novel by British author Frank Baker, with a similar story line, which preceded du Maurier's tale by some fifteen years. Before that, Britisher Philip MacDonald plotted a like narrative in "Our Feathered Friends." The core concept of MacDonald's story is that the benevolent countenance of Mother Nature is a mask, behind which lies a terrible visage, that of Hecate the death crone, if you will. Mother's wrathful persona is manifested by earthquakes and superstorms, but perhaps is most unnerving when it takes the form of a murderous wild animal. It awakens ancestral fears of a time when humans were more likely prey than predator.

Inexplicable rampages by wild animals do, in fact, occur in real life, as well as in fiction. One such episode attracted global attention in 1898, when a pair of maneless male Af-

9

rican lions appeared seemingly out of nowhere to slaughter and devour some three dozen workers who were building a railroad over the red earth of Kenya's Tsavo region. Night after night, for almost a year, the "maneaters of Tsavo" entered railroad camps, where they ripped sleeping workers out of their tents and dragged them screaming into the bush. The lions ate with such gusto that the surviving workers, huddled under canvas, could hear the crunching of their friends' bones in the dark. Morning light revealed the meal's leftovers: limbs, heads, and pieces of gory flesh strewn among the acacia shrubs. No one had ever seen these lions before the attacks began, nor was the reason for their depredations ever determined, even after they were shot and killed.

Appropriately, *Tsavo* means "place of slaughter" in the local Kamba tongue. The gruesome name stems not from the lions but from a time when fierce Maasai warriors stained the already red soil with Kamba blood. More than once, Tsavo has been a killing ground. It may be my overly active imagination, but I have walked places among the coal-black, cindery lava cones of Tsavo's Chyulu Hills that made the hair on the back of my neck prickle, or at least made me inescapably uneasy. And apparently I am not the only person who has felt this way. Local tradition has it that an aura of evil hangs over parts of the region. Indeed, the Swahili word for one of the stark volcanic cones and lava flow that are among the dominant features of the Tsavo landscape is *Shetani,* a name for malevolent spirits.

The incident of the man-killing Tsavo lions is eerily similar to a spate of attacks by their smaller American namesake that lasted for more than a decade in a California state park. It is an episode pertinent to the subject of this book, because the potential increasingly exists for something like it occurring again elsewhere, perhaps on the outskirts of a city near you. Mountain lions—or cougars, as they are referred to in this book—inhabiting Cuyamaca Rancho State Park, only forty miles from San Diego, went on a rampage, targeting people in an inexplicable manner eerily evocative of the Tsavo lions. Biologists were at a loss to explain a blitz of attacks by the cougars on hikers and campers, resorting instead to terms such as "weird," "unexpected," and "rare." And as with Hitchcock's birds, the attacks were sporadic; the cougars seemed to suspend their aggressive activity while a nervous populace took a deep breath. Before anyone could exhale, however, the attacks resumed. Said the park's supervising ranger at the time, "The lions are behaving in a way we historically did not think they would. I've been involved with this issue for two years, and I wish I had answers" (*Los Angeles Times,* December 13, 1994).

The problem became so acute that twice, in action virtually unprecedented, the park was closed to visitors. Campgrounds were emptied and rangers combed trails to round up and evacuate hikers. All told, cougars menaced people at least sixteen times, with authorities killing eleven of the cats. According to accepted thinking, cougars that stalk people likely are sick, aged, or otherwise too incapacitated to hunt deer or other large natural prey. None of the cougars involved in incidents at the park were infirm. All were in the prime of health, easily able to hunt victims of their choice.

Whatever the reason, cougars in the park became unusually bold beginning in June 1988, when two of them chased after a couple with a small child. Park rangers shot both cats. In September 1993, a cougar loped after two horseback riders for a half mile. Time after time, cougars threatened people in different parts of the park, sometimes stalking them outright, leaving no doubt their intentions were predatory. Tragically, one stalk, in December 1994, was successful, ending in the death of a hiker. The victim was fifty-five-year-old Iris Kenna, a counselor at a San Diego high school. Trackers chased down and shot the killer cougar, which was the fifth executed for menacing people in the park within only a fifteen-month period. Jeff Weir, assistant deputy director for the state Department of Fish and Game, somewhat understated the case when he made the following comment to reporters: "Cuyamaca is a hot spot for cougars. There are several others, but Cuyamaca is the hottest" (*Los Angeles Times,* December 13, 1994). He could not explain why.

Two years later, game wardens killed another cougar in the park after it charged a woman on horseback and then came after them. Two years after that, authorities killed four cougars that had been menacing people and dogs at a campsite. The attacks had ceased by 2000, but visitors are still urged not to hike or otherwise travel park trails alone.

Although parts of Cuyamaca are rugged, with oak and pine forests and elevations of five thousand feet, it is not a wilderness that is remote from civilization. It lies within the San Diego metropolitan area. A half-million visitors tramp its trails and use its campgrounds annually. The mountainous area in which it lies is dotted with pretty tourist towns, such as Julian and Alpine, within commuting distance of downtown San Diego. Cougars as well as humans make the commute, and the cats now prowl San Diego's suburbs almost as regularly as the middle-aged human females who are nicknamed for them stalk the city's downtown clubs.

Encroachment by cougars on the urbs is not unique to San Diego. Cougars are edging close to civilization in many parts of North America. So are bears, supersize coyotes with wolf blood in their veins, and several other species of wild creatures once confined to wilderness and backwaters. Make no mistake about it. Potentially dangerous wildlife is invading human turf, entering backyards in suburban neighborhoods, prowling urban parks, and stalking city streets. Big, powerful wild beasts are in the garden and on the doorstep. They are not the benign beings of feel-good nature shows. They bite, scratch, and sometimes kill. They crash into cars and through store windows. They invade homes, sometimes by accident, other times in search of food. They scare the wits out of parents and pet owners, especially those never before exposed to the often-bloody reality of nature in the raw. They snatch pets out of backyards and eye children hungrily. They leave their droppings on lawns. They rattle among the landscape plantings and slither out of swamps to the edges of backyard swimming pools. Fang and claw have crossed the white picket fence.

Wildlife biologists and government officials trying to balance the needs of man and beast must now operate according to a whole new set of rules. Municipalities and their resi dents whose exposure to "problem wildlife" once consisted of raccoons raiding garbage cans and Canada geese pooping on putting greens now need contend with creatures that may view a child playing in the backyard as prey.

A headline in the online *Science Daily,* October 5, 2012, proclaimed what many wildlife experts and a good portion of the citizenry already knew: "Urban Coyotes Could Be Setting the Stage for Larger Carnivores—Wolves, Bears and Mountain Lions—To Move into Cities." The story accompanying the headline described a study of urban coyotes in the Chicago area begun by Ohio State researcher Stan Gehrt in 2000. "It amazes me," said Gehrt, an associate professor of environment and natural resources, about how the two thousand coyotes in the Chicago area make a living amidst a metropolitan population of nine million humans.

Gehrt, quoted in the article, called the coyote a "test case" for bigger, badder predators that are appearing on the urban scene. Indeed, a sign of things to come for Chicago— and elsewhere in the eastern half of the nation—grabbed headlines in 2008. In true Windy City fashion, police gunned down a 150-pound male cougar cornered in an alley in the Roscoe Village neighborhood on the North Side. Forensics later determined it had wandered east from South Dakota's Black Hills.

Gehrt summed up the outlook for urban and suburban dwellers this way for the science news outlet: "It used to be rural areas where we would have this challenge of coexistence versus conflict with carnivores. In the future, and I would say currently, it's cities where we're going to have this intersection between people and carnivores." He went on to say: "We used to think only little carnivores could live in cities, and even then we thought they couldn't really achieve large numbers. But we're finding that these animals are much more flexible than we gave them credit for and they're adjusting to our cities. That's going to put the burden back on us: Are we going to be able to adjust to them living with us or are we not going to be able to coexist?" Answering his own question, Gehrt said, in effect, "Get used to it." The big bad wolf has come calling and intends to stay. Rick Winslow, a carnivore biologist with the New Mexico Department of Game and Fish, could have been talking about almost any part of the land and a variety of species when, after a cougar killed a man in the Silver City region, said, "Attacks by wildlife may become more frequent as our growing population expands into the urban-wildlife interface" (press release, New Mexico Department of Game and Fish, June 23, 2008).

This book focuses on the increasing chance of conflict between people and creatures that—by virtue of size, habit, or other attributes—are dangerous or potentially so. The odds of conflict are mounting day by day. Perhaps never before have so many such creatures inhabited such densely concentrated populations of humans. Even the nation's epic metropolis is experiencing a surge in new forms of wildlife. It was only 1984 when I wrote in my book, *The New York City Wildlife*

Guide, "The mammals that regularly inhabit the city . . . are smaller than whitetail deer, ranging in size from shrews that could fit into the palm of your hand to raccoons and foxes." The Big Apple's fauna now include a growing deer herd. New York's Finest have chased white-tailed deer bounding across the concrete backyards of the Bronx's Belmont, the borough's Little Italy. A whitetail herd thrives on Staten Island, which still has considerable open space but is by no means Maine. Coyotes, long emblematic of the West, have invaded the eastern megalopolis as well. The predators prowling Central Park after dark now include *Canis latrans* var. in addition to *Homo sapiens.* Eastern coyotes, which have populated regions hitherto foreign to them, may represent a significantly greater threat than their smaller western kin. As a famed Canadian wild-canid specialist told me several years ago and many biologists today have verified, they have acquired wolf genes while edging their way eastward through Canada. And they have proven they will stalk and kill a human.

In a dramatic "who'd have thunk?" development, hunters now legally pursue bears in Bergen County, New Jersey, the western gateway to the George Washington Bridge. The twenty-first century began with bear hunts sanctioned by the Garden State. Connecticut, from which black bears vanished early in the nineteenth century, now has so many bruins it is considering a bear hunt. Black bears, which many misguided people view as real-life teddy bears, are responsible for more human deaths than the grizzly, and one shot in a recent New Jersey bear hunt weighed in the neighborhood of eight hundred pounds, well within the grizzly's size range.

The story in the East is no different than elsewhere across the country. Deer and coyotes no longer cause a stir when they cross the lawns of mansions in Shaker Heights, Ohio, a posh suburb bordering Cleveland. Deer, of course, are not generally considered harmful to humans—unless they're encountered on the roadway, when said humans are behind the wheel of a car. So many collisions between vehicles and deer occur that insurance companies keep a tally. Hit a moose and the results are usually catastrophic. Moose collisions are no longer confined to roads through the wild woods of Maine or Montana. Recently, a moose trashed a car on crowded Interstate 95, between New York City and Boston, in Old Saybrook, Connecticut.

"It's an urban jungle out there," wrote Joe Baird of the *Salt Lake Tribune* in an article dated October 22, 2006, describing how the Salt Lake City metro area now hosts moose, mountain lions, bears, rattlesnakes, and other animals once confined to the hinterlands. "Brazen Wild Animals Moving In On Our Turf," proclaimed an article on New York City's WCBS.com in the same year.

The year 2006 seemed big on such stories, as the media began to recognize the problem. With "animals everywhere" wrote Heather Park of the online *Colorado Daily,* "a walk around Boulder can be . . . risky, including encounters with deer, mountain lions and bears" (May 27, 2006).

This book will explore the great environmental Mixmaster that has churned up such a volatile brew of humans and beasts. The irony of wildlife's intrusion upon landscapes engineered and inhabited by humans is inescapable. Year after year, even hour by hour, it seems, conservationists—I am one—drone on about the escalating loss of biodiversity as species slide toward extinction because of human activities. Iconic beasts that seemed eternal, such as the African lion, are disappearing from their wild habitats. Yet it is in large part due to humans, in addition to the adaptability of some species, that many types of wildlife have multiplied, and even expanded their geographical range.

It is a great paradox of our time. Subdivisions are replacing wild lands. Cities are as crowded as ever. Endangered-species lists grow longer. Yet people seem to be increasingly encountering threatening animals, often large animals. This book will look at what's behind this seeming contradiction. The situation is more complicated than merely the fact that people are settling down in animal habitat, although that is a key part of the puzzle. In part, it recalls the old saying, "Be careful what you wish for." Starting in the 1970s, "urban wildlife" was a buzzword among conservationists and wildlife biologists. Projects to improve wildlife habitat in human population centers was a path toward grant money. Urban-wildlife restoration is one of the factors leading to the rise of the backyard jungle that is the subject of this book. Both humans and wildlife now inhabit this jungle, and we're going to have to figure out how to keep the peace.

The list of sometimes-unwelcome animals sharing space with humans goes beyond mammals. Indeed, the quintessential species that has come back from the brink with a vengeance is the American alligator. Alligators, in fact, led the invasion. They were among the first large creatures to show up in urban and suburban locales where no beasts like them had ever gone before. Parts of the South are swarming with alligators, not that many decades ago considered an endangered species.

The perspective I bring to the subject of alligator-human conflicts is that of one who might be called an unindicted co-conspirator. I was a New York Zoological Society (now Wildlife Conservation Society) curator, and representative to the American Alligator Council, which during the 1960s was a major force leading to laws protecting the species. When I wrote a book for young people on the endangered American alligator back then, I never dreamed that within a few decades gators would be back in droves, and not just in swamps but in golf course ponds and backyard boat canals.

The same is true of constricting snakes, some so big they can, and do, swallow alligators. Giant tropical constrictors, chiefly the Burmese python, now live and breed in and around the Florida Everglades and threaten to expand their range, especially if global warming continues. These reptiles constitute a somewhat special case, because they are introduced alien species, originating as captives released by irresponsible pet owners. The problems they pose, however, are the same as those created by native species impinging on human habitat. Venomous snakes, perhaps impacted by the warming climate and moving into new territory, are also making their way to the doorstep, and even crossing the threshold.

So if you're thinking about relocating, before buying a new home you might want to search for news about wildlife encounters while you're checking out an area's schools and cultural amenities. Several years ago, while picking up mail at the country store that serves as our post office, I encountered a woman who had just moved to our small Connecticut town from New York City, a hundred miles away. The lady was worried because she had just seen something four-legged and furry lying dead by the roadside. The roadkill probably was a raccoon. "Did you know," she asked breathlessly, "that there are *wild animals* around here?" I haven't seen her since. Perhaps she is back in Manhattan. The encounter happened sufficiently long ago that coyotes were still rare, and bears only a rumor, in my part of Connecticut. Nowadays in my town, if something upends your trashcan in the night it is as likely to be a black bear as a coon.

While some people react to their new animal neighbors with horror, nature lovers and wildlife buffs find it exciting, at times thrilling. When a pack of coywolves erupts into full nocturnal cry from the darkened woods abutting my home, sounding like hellhounds unleashed, my hackles rise but my spirit soars at the aura of the wild at my doorstep. I experienced the same primal thrill when I heard for the first time the swelling thunder of lions rolling over the night-cloaked African savanna. Now the call of the wild is just outside my window. The same sound makes other people in my area check their door locks. Either way, it's a jungle out there. Our backyard comfort zone has been breached. In this book you'll learn how the animal invasion of our domain started, why it is continuing, and what to do about it—because we *can* live safely, even enjoyably, in the new animal kingdom, even if it includes beasts that occasionally view us as lunch.

CHAPTER 1

THE BIG CAT IS BACK:
Return of the Cougar

After decades of denial, federal and state wildlife agencies finally concede that cougars are returning to territory they vacated long ago in the eastern half of the nation. There really was no official cabal to cover up the fact that cougars were prowling places they were not supposed to be, as some cougar junkies and conspiracy theorists believe. Even so, state wildlife agencies and the U.S. Fish and Wildlife Service were reluctant to accept that the big cat is back in its former haunts.

While in some regions cougars may never be more than fleeting visitors, they are multiplying in western North America and steadily reclaiming their old turf in the eastern half of the continent, turning up and causing a ruckus even in New England. The skeptics who dissed cougar sightings east of the Rockies were silenced by a research paper published in June 2012 in the Wildlife Society's prestigious *Journal of Wildlife Management*. It left no doubt that cougars were reclaiming their former territory, and even reproducing in some areas from which they were extirpated a century ago. "Cougars Are Recolonizing the Midwest," the research paper proclaimed, while noting that the cats are roving even farther east, to Connecticut and New York. Earning broad media coverage, and recognized as the first in-depth analysis of statistics on cougar sightings in places where their existence had been disputed, the study was led by a wildlife ecologist at Southern Illinois University, Dr. Clay Nielsen. He is also scientific director of the Cougar Network, a nonprofit conservation group.

"The cougar population declined dramatically from 1900, due to hunting and lack of prey, leaving the remaining population isolated to the American West," said Nielsen's coauthor Michelle LaRue, quoted in a June 14, 2012, press release announcing the study. "We present the hard evidence that the western population has spread, with cougar populations re-establishing across the Midwest," she added, without rebuttal from biologists who had earlier refused to accept the cougar resurgence. The LaRue-Nielson study covered fourteen states and Canadian provinces east of the Rocky Mountains. Cougars had been absent from some of them for as much as a century. The authors of the study maintain it reveals a trend "reversing 100 years of species decline due to loss of habitat and other factors."

The cougar comeback is bound to increase interactions with people. Nielsen recognized this trend when he warned, as quoted in a separate press release on the study findings, "Public and wildlife managers may need to deal with increasing cougar populations in the future if re-colonization continues."

Publication of the LaRue-Nielsen study forced the scientific community to place its imprimatur on a conclusion that a host of ordinary people had reached years before: wild cougars once again roam the eastern half of North America. The study ended the frustration of assorted hunters, hikers, birders, law enforcement officers, joggers, and suburban housewives in virtually every state and province east of the Rockies, who for years had reported seeing cougars, not just in forest and field but in backyards, only to be told by authorities that what they'd really seen were dogs, bobcats, shadows, or phantoms. If the cougar sighting was confirmed, it was said to be an escaped captive, an explanation that was a real stretch, virtually requiring that pet cougars are as abundant as gerbils.

I have been keeping tabs on cougar sightings in the eastern United States since the 1960s, when I worked as a curator for the New York Zoological Society, with offices at the Bronx Zoo. My interest began when a resident of rural northern New Jersey supplied a zoo mammalogist with a photograph of large tracks in the snow, taken near his home. Zoo experts huddled over the photo, then identified the prints as those of a cougar. The decision was made to keep quiet about the photograph so as not to spark a panic or get would-be cougar hunters up in arms. Around the same period of time, I was visiting with a true modern-day mountain man, a friend of my father-in-law's, a physician who treated mountain people in rural East Tennessee. Bear hunter Dayton Hill lived with his bear- and hog-dogs about four thousand feet up in the Smoky Mountains. Dayton told me that he kept bells on his cows so he could hear them moving if they were agitated during the night by "panthers." The woods-wise mountaineer did not mean bobcats.

For decades, the response from state and federal wildlife agencies to cougar sightings outside the West followed the party line about misidentification or errant pets. Almost begrudgingly, they began to add a third possibility: lone wanderers straying far from concentrated cougar populations in the western states. The revised response was sparked by the 2008 appearance of the South Dakota cougar in Chicago, and even more dramatically, in June 2011, when a mountain lion prowled among the mansions of hedge fund managers and CEOs in opulent Greenwich, Connecticut, thirty miles from Manhattan. At first, officials dismissed the sightings, then opted for the "escaped pet" explanation. That argument was trashed, a week or so later, when a 140-pound male cougar was struck and killed by an SUV on the Wilbur Cross Parkway, in Milford, thirty-five miles from Greenwich. Genetic tests proved, hands down, that the two animals were one and the same, and that the "Milford mountain lion" was a wild western migrant.

"The journey of this mountain lion is a testament to the wonders of nature and the tenacity and adaptability of this species," pronounced Daniel C. Esty, commissioner of the Connecticut Department of Energy and Environmental Protection (DEEP), which manages the state's wildlife. As quoted in a July 26, 2011, DEEP press release, he added: "The conformation of a wild mountain lion in our state was the first recorded in more than 100 years." Esty quickly stressed that "there is still no evidence indicating that there is a native population of mountain lions in Connecticut."

Esty's wildlife division chief, Rick Jacobson, a highly respected and practical wildlife scientist, agreed. Connecticut, Jacobson told me, simply lacks sufficient territory for a breeding population of cougars, so at most, the state might see a few transients. Connecticut's DEEP continued this line after, late in January 2013, the building inspector of the town of East Lyme, on the shore of Long Island Sound, reported seeing a cougar cross the road in front of his house one evening. After his dog began barking frantically, the inspector said, he looked outside and saw two yellowish-green eyes in the dark. Illuminated by a streetlight, he said, a cougar crossed the road.

The DEEP's response: "There has not been a native population in the state for quite some time and no verified sighting in over 100 years, with the exception of the one that was killed on the Merritt Parkway back in June 2011. But in the absence of verifiable evidence (confirmed photographs, samples of scat, etc.) we continue to believe that there is no breeding populations of mountain lions in Connecticut"

(DEEP spokesman Dwayne Gardner, quoted in *Greenwich Patch,* February 1, 2013).

Since 1972, I have lived in the lower Connecticut River valley, an area that, while not exactly untamed wilderness, has a considerable amount of open space in the form of state forests and parks, watershed, and private hunting preserves. Right down to 2012, when an animal control officer in a neighboring town reported seeing a cougar, I have been told again and again by people that they had seen one of these cats. Residents of one housing development in my town claim they have had a cougar hanging around their holdings for years, often sitting on a large rock near the backyard of a McMansion.

I have not seen that cougar or any other around my town, but I have heard and observed signs of their passing. A few years back, a hunter I know, who lives in an enclave within a state forest a few miles from my home, told me that he had heard a cougar calling from the woods on three successive nights. A week later, I heard the cry myself, from the woodland next to my house, first loud, then fading into the distance. The sound was consistent with the classic description of a cougar call: like a woman screaming in terror. During the winter of 2010–11, I found unusual tracks in the snow covering my small market garden. The prints were not those of a bear, and obviously feline. I have seen bobcats back of my home, but the tracks were too large and too widely spaced to be left by one of them. They were, it appeared, those of a cougar. Two days later, on the woods road bordering my land, where coyotes regularly chase deer, I found scat full of deer hair. It was not coyote scat but seemingly that of a cougar—and at the risk of sounding scatological, I know my animal signs well enough to be listed as the consultant on a National Audubon Society guidebook to animal tracks.

As to whether Connecticut has a breeding population

of cougars, who really knows? "Connecticut" is a political, not geographical, entity. If there was a breeding population to the north, say in Vermont or New Hampshire, my home could well be within easy wandering range. So whether or not the cats breed within the political boundaries of the state, it could still be considered cougar country.

As cougars continue to materialize out of nowhere in places that have been without them for generations, the debate over whether they are strays or natives will increase. Either way, there is plenty of room within their original range for them to reoccupy. The cougar has the largest original range, spanning the broadest spectrum of ecological zones, of any living land mammal in the New World. At the time of European arrival in the Americas, cougar country covered both New World continents from the subarctic boreal forest to the southern tip of South America, where the Andes Mountains, at that point little more than hills, descend into the chill subantarctic waters. Not surprisingly, over such a vast area, in which many languages are spoken and many cultures exist, people have given the cougar many different names. In English or English corruptions of other tongues alone, there are about forty in all. The word *cougar* itself results from an etymological evolution. According to the Cougar Fund, a conservation organization based in Wyoming, it originated in the word *susuarana,* which in the language of South America's Tupi Amerindians means "false deer." The Portuguese in Brazil converted it to *cuguacurrana,* which was shortened to *cuougar* by an eighteenth-century French naturalist, which English speakers scrambled into its present form. Among its other names: mountain lion, catamount, panther, Mexican lion, mountain screamer, puma, painter, deer tiger, Indian devil, and catawampus.

There is no true scientific count of cougar numbers throughout this vast territory, but estimates range as high as fifty thousand animals, of which thirty thousand live in North America. A quick mention of some of the different habitats that cougars inhabit reveals their ecological adaptability. They prowl the peat islands of the Okefenokee Swamp in Georgia, the wooded strands of the Florida Everglades, and the swamps of Venezuela's Orinoco Delta. They hunt deer in the deciduous woods of Missouri and the rainforests of Central America, as well as on the plains of Montana and the Argentinian pampas. Their eerie cries echo among the peaks of the Canadian Rockies and over the windswept altiplano, the bleak high plateau of the Andes. They tread the Grand Canyon of Arizona as well as the brushy canyons of suburbs around San Diego, San Francisco, and within the city limits of Los Angeles.

Reaching their largest size at the northern and southern extremes of their range, cougars can top 250 pounds, especially males. Generally, cougars average less than 160 pounds, although 180-pound males are not unusual, and reach a length of nine feet, about four feet of which is tail. Size wise, the cougar is a big cat, although it is more closely related to small cats than to lions, tigers, jaguars, and leopards. It lacks the specialized larynx that enables the true big cats to roar. The cougar's call is best described by one of the names given to it by frontiersmen: the screamer.

While cougars can subsist on a diet of small prey, even insects and fish, their size enables them to hunt larger mammals. In the Andes foothills, they stalk guanaco, wild ancestors of the llama; on the high plateau, they hunt vicunas, wild progenitors of alpacas. Through much of South America, however, and in all of North America, their dietary mainstay is deer, several species of which exist in one part or another of the cat's range. Cougars hunt small pudu deer in the Andes and swamp deer in Amazon forests. From the Rocky Mountains west, mule deer are an important prey. Except for the

Great Basin region and Pacific Coast, however, the key prey of the cougar in North America, and into northern South America, as well, is the white-tailed deer. Persecution aside, the abundance and territory occupied by the cougar waxes and wanes with that of white-tailed deer. Burgeoning populations of whitetails throughout most of their North American range, in fact, may be the key to why cougars are fanning out from their western sanctuaries.

Given the adaptability and the immense range of geography and habitats occupied by the cougar, it seems logical, in an evolutionary context, that the species would have branched into many subspecies, each suited to its specific environment. Indeed, until recently, that was the conclusion of taxonomists, scientists whose job it is to identify species and assign them positions on the tree of life. Taxonomists, however, like to reclassify, probably because it keeps them in business.

Traditionally, scientists divided cougars into thirty-two subspecies, each assigned to a different geographic area. The traditional classification was based largely on easily recognizable physical differences as well as where the animals lived. These included differences in size—the largest cougars are those in the northern and southern, thus coolest, portions of its range—and bone structure. The Florida subspecies, for example, has stiffer, shorter fur and a broader skull than the others. It is smaller in overall size, with smaller feet, than cougars of northern climes, where wide feet are an asset in the snow. The signature difference of the Florida panther is something no other cougar has: a distinctly arched nasal bone that gives it a Roman nose.

When techniques were developed that enabled scientists to decipher genomes and explore cougars genetically, the picture changed. The genetics study that challenged and eventually overcame the traditional view was by scientists at the

National Cancer Institute's Laboratory of Genomic Diversity in Frederick, Maryland. Reported at a meeting in 1999 of the American Genetic Association, it was published the next year in the *Journal of Heredity.* Analysis of DNA from all of the thirty-two so-called subspecies indicated that, genetically, there are but six of them, although cougars in Florida, referred to there as panthers, may constitute a seventh. Geographic features, such as mountain ranges, serve as partial barriers between the different subspecies, but not enough to discourage hanky-panky between individuals living on the edges, so genes are occasionally exchanged between the groups.

The genetic pruning of the cougar family tree met with some resistance from traditionalists, as often happens in science, but earned acceptance by most. It is used by organizations such as the International Union for Conservation of Nature (IUCN), the world's oldest and largest environmental network, which maintains the global Red List of Threatened Species.

Under the revised classification, South America has four subspecies: the eastern *(Puma concolor capricornensis),* northern *(P. c. concolor),* southern *(P. c. puma),* and Argentine *(P. c. cabreae).* The Costa Rican cougar ranges Central America; the cougar with the largest range, the North American *(P. c. cougar),* from British Columbia to the Mexican tropics. Strong evidence suggests that the Florida panther, which barely survives in the wild, is also a distinct subspecies *(P. c. corryi).*

Research on cougar genetics based on the new taxonomy suggests that about eight million years ago, a cougar ancestor migrated from Asia across the Bering land bridge between Alaska and Siberia. This now-submerged landmass was high and dry when seawater was locked up in glaciers and sea level dropped during the Pleistocene ice ages. Later, during what zoogeographers call the Great American Interchange, when volcanism shoved the Isthmus of Panama above the sea, the prehistoric cougar moved into South America. The Interchange, which peaked about three million years ago, was a time when a multitude of species from North and South America engaged in bustling two-way traffic across the isthmus.

South America may have served as a refuge for the cougar after the great extinction of large terrestrial North American mammals at the end of the Pleistocene in North America between ten thousand and twelve thousand years ago. So suggests the study published in the *Journal of Heredity,* led by Dr. Melanie Culver, later an assistant professor of wildlife and fisheries at the University of Arizona. The cougar, according to Culver, may have vanished from North America along with the sabertoothed cat, mastodon, and other great Pleistocene mammals. The fact that all living North American cougars display a high level of genetic similarity, she says, indicates that they recently descended from a small, common ancestral group. This group, she figures, consisted of migrants from South America filling the vacuum in the North after the Pleistocene. Apparently, then as now, cougars readily move back into territory they have previously vacated, if given the chance.

The conclusion reached by Culver and her colleagues— that only one subspecies of cougar has inhabited North America in recent times—lent great irony to an announcement by the U.S. Fish and Wildlife Service on March 2, 2011. Hoping to end years of controversy, and with considerable fanfare, the federal agency proclaimed in a press release that the "eastern cougar" subspecies was extinct and thus could be removed from the federal endangered-species list. If one accepts the new genetic classification of cougars, the service has delisted a cat that never was. Genetically, there was no eastern cougar, according to the new research. However, the USFWS ignored the new taxonomy when it sounded the death knell of the eastern cougar, leading the *New York Times*, on March 2, 2011, to headline, "Eastern Cougar Is Declared Extinct. With an Asterisk." The *Times* noted that scientists are inclined to believe it never was a true subspecies. Christened the "gray ghost" of the Northeast, the eastern cougar was supposed to be a subspecies in its own right. Establishment biologists claimed the last eastern cougars vanished in the 1930s due to persecution and near-extermination of white-tailed deer, their main prey. Not everyone agreed they were extinct. A coterie of armchair cougar experts and cougar-friendly organizations, such as the Eastern Puma Research Network, held firm in their belief that repeated sightings down through the years were of eastern cougars. Their cause was championed by noted Canadian wildlife biologist Bruce Wright, who long maintained that cougars persisted in the Northeast as a breeding population.

Fueling a conspiracy theory, the USFWS asserted that cougar sightings in the supposed former range of the eastern cougar were not of the ghost cat but of escapees belonging to other species. A USFWS blog posting on the day the extinction designation was made declared, "You may have seen a cougar in the East, but it wasn't an eastern cougar." The response hewed to the old line, issued often over the years, that such sightings were "cougars of other subspecies, often South American subspecies, that had been held in captivity and had escaped or been released to the wild." As if hedging its bets, the agency eventually conceded that some sightings just might be "wild cougars of the western United States subspecies that had migrated eastward into the Midwest." The agency never mentioned that if this was indeed the case, and according to the new classification, the North American subspecies was merely reclaiming its old haunts. Two months after these statements, the Milford mountain lion showed that migrants were not only entering the Midwest but had reached the East Coast. The research paper on cougar re-colonization cited the Connecticut cougar incident. Quoted in a press release announcing the study, coauthor Michelle LaRue noted that while the distance covered by the Milford mountain lion was a rare example, "We found that cougars are roaming long distances and are moving back into portions of their historical range."

The Milford cougar was indeed a wild individual that had traveled fifteen hundred miles from its DNA-proven original home in the Black Hills of South Dakota. The wandering beast, it turned out, had previously been tracked in Minnesota, where it was called the St. Croix mountain lion. The link to Minnesota was made by tests of scat, blood, and hair left there in the snow during 2009 and 2010. The Black Hills where the animal originated turned out to be the core of three major cougar populations that seem to be sending out émigrés on a regular basis. Two cougars found in Missouri during 2011 were from the Black Hills. So was the cougar killed in Chicago, which traveled more than a thousand miles to its death at the hands of Chicago cops. Scientists say the cougars exiting the Black Hills are from an over-flowing population that has passed the saturation point, a remarkable turn of affairs given that by the 1970s the species was considered almost extinct in South Dakota; in 1978 it was granted legal protection. Proof of how quickly cougars can reestablish themselves is that by 2005 the state opened a hunting season on the cats, with an allowed take of twenty-five animals, to control their numbers. The Black Hills population, which reached about 140 breeding adults in a matter of a decade or so, first overflowed into Nebraska, forming a resident population numbering a couple of dozen animals now holed up in the northwestern part of the state.

The first confirmed cougar in Nebraska was in 1991, when one was killed by a hunter. By 2007, a female and her kittens were photographed. By 2012 almost seventy sightings had been confirmed. Nebraska had the highest number of cougar sightings—sixty-seven—included in the analytical study by LaRue and Nielsen. Among the other states, Missouri had ten sightings, Arkansas eight, Illinois three, and Iowa four. There have been many more sightings in those states besides those mentioned in the study. During the first half of 2012, authorities in Missouri confirmed fourteen reports, two more than in the previous sixteen years. Examination of cougars that turned up in Missouri indicated that they, in turn, had overflowed from Nebraska.

Part of the reason cougars are fanning out is that they are true loners, requiring a home range of up to 150 square miles. Male cougars instinctively start to wander at about a year of age. By checking out of their home territories, they escape larger, older males that might kill them to eliminate competition. As well, moving away prevents inbreeding with close female relatives.

The western states in general are the wellspring of the cougar spillover, just as South America was the source of North American cougars after the ice ages. Canada, according to the University of Victoria, British Columbia, has about four thousand cougars, a quarter of which inhabit Vancouver Island, which probably has the highest concentration anywhere. "Western cougar populations have been increasing since the 1960s," notes the Cougar Network on its website, largely due to expanded populations of deer and elk. In many states, the population of cougars has increased from hundreds to thousands since the 1960s. In the Cougar Network's estimation, "the species is beginning to recolonize the adjacent Prairie States."

In 2007, a novel reason for the abundance of deer and elk,

and subsequent multiplication of cougars, was put forth by Darcy Whiteside of Alberta's Ministry of Environment and Sustainable Resource Development: climate change. Warm winters boost the populations of deer, elk, and moose, thus contributing to cougar survival in the province, Whiteside has suggested.

Cougars are flourishing even more in California, where their population has tripled, to more than five thousand animals since the species was protected and hunting banned in 1971. At the same time, the state's human population has been doubling every twenty-five years. The resurgence of the cougar was first seen in California, giving credence to the notion that, as Jay Leno has pointed out, all fads—and trends—begin in the Golden State. As California's human population has grown, shopping centers and developments have encroached on cougar territory while the cats have increased in number. As a result, the odds of cat and human encounters have increased astronomically.

Until 1986, the only cougar attacks reported in North America during the twentieth century were two in California during July 1909. Both were by the same rabid animal. Since 1986, when a five-year-old boy was injured in an Orange County park, attacks in North America have occurred with unnerving regularity; by 2012, there had been more than a dozen in California alone.

Like Cuyamaca Rancho, state parks and other preserves are often the settings for cougar attacks because they attract both cats and people. Deer and other animals that cougars prey upon often follow the same trails as human visitors. Whiting Ranch Wilderness Park is in the Santa Ana Mountains, with considerable wild land. It is also in Mission Viejo, a master-planned city of almost one hundred thousand people in Orange County, California, ringed by cheek-by-jowl housing developments. The park is especially attractive to mountain bikers, some of whom have been attacked. In 2004 Anne Hjelle, a thirty-year-old fitness instructor and former Marine, was jumped from the brush by a cougar as she pedaled through a park. Typical of a cougar attacking prey, it grabbed her head in its jaws. Companion bikers threw rocks and a bike at the animal, while one of them held on to Hjelle's leg until the big cat released its grip on her head, which witnesses said was completely engulfed in the cougar's jaws. The biker was critically injured but survived. Had she died, it would have been the second person killed by the same cougar that day. Officials said footprints and human tissue taken from the cat's stomach after authorities shot it verified that the same animal earlier attacked and killed a thirty-five-year-old cyclist, Mark Reynolds, whose body was found partially buried near his disabled bike. Authorities believe the cougar attacked Reynolds as he was replacing a broken chain, then concealed him after consuming part of his body. He died only a few hundred yards from large housing developments in what a news account described as "a gruesome reminder of the danger that exists when suburban sprawl encroaches on the wilderness" (*USA Today,* January 9, 2004).

Commenting on the Whiting Ranch attacks in a *San Francisco Chronicle* article on January 10, 2004, cougar researcher Walter Boyce, a veterinarian at the University of California at Davis, summed up why people are increasingly coming into conflict with cougars and, importantly, so many other potentially dangerous wild creatures: "We're in their habitat. The more people are close, the more chance for interaction."

The same news account quoted Steve Torres, an environmental scientist at the Department of Fish and Game, who said of the attack, "We should expect to have some level of it continuing to happen, because it is related to humans and lions interfacing, and that is continuing to increase."

Indeed, human interactions with cougars happen with increasing frequency in California's urban settings. Cougars have been seen along Interstate 5 near Sacramento; at a Modesto high school in broad daylight; on golf courses and in backyards in suburban Los Angeles. In May 2012, police in Santa Monica were forced to shoot a ninety-pound young male cougar in the courtyard of a downtown office building. The creature's DNA indicated it had not come from a population in the nearby Santa Monica Mountains, as suspected, but from a group of cougars farther to the north. It was the first cougar seen in the city in thirty years. Not far from where the Santa Monica cougar was shot, its conspecifics seem to regularly frequent the four-thousand-plus acres of Griffith Park, which contains some rugged landscapes but nevertheless lies within urban Los Angeles. Biologists captured one there in March 2012, then released it with a GPS collar so they could track its movements. It was the second cougar discovered there in less than a decade.

As the killing of the cougar in Chicago demonstrates, urban and suburban incidents are not confined to California. In April 2011, police officers in Richland, Washington, killed a cougar that had entered the basement of a home. They shot the animal only after failing to sedate it with a tranquilizer dart.

The more cougars enter centers of human population, the greater the chance they will become home invaders. A hungry cougar chased a dog through a pet door into a home near Salida, Colorado, on a March afternoon in 2010 while a mother and her two young children sat at a kitchen table. They ran into a bedroom where another child was sleeping and called police. Meanwhile, the cougar battled the family's five small dogs. The cougar was eventually shot with a tranquilizer dart and died. In August 2004, a cougar entered a couple's home in Ute Pass, Colorado, in what turned out to be an episode that bordered on the humorous but could have been terribly tragic. Authorities suspect that the cougar entered the home because it was attracted to the couple's toddler crying himself to sleep. Once inside, in a bedroom, it apparently was distracted by the wife's slipper. The husband, sleepy-eyed after being awakened from a nap, confronted the cat as it was chewing on the slipper. Fortunately for all concerned, it backed away and padded from the house, carrying the stolen footwear. In June 2008, a New Mexico man was killed by a cougar as he stood outside his home near Silver City, a university town of thirty thousand people. His partly eaten body was found sixty feet away, where the cougar cached it under a ledge for a second meal.

The fact that cougars show up in western towns and cities does not necessarily mean that breeding populations exist within municipal limits of all. However, many western cities, even large metro areas such as Los Angeles, lie close to vast tracts of wild country, with more than enough space to support native cougar population. So, in effect, the cougars that visit Griffith Park are natives.

While rural countryside rings some of the metropolises of the East, it is not nearly as remote or wild as, say, the outskirts of Denver or even Phoenix. This mitigates against establishment of breeding cougar populations near, for example, the I-95 corridor between Washington, D.C., and Boston. However, the suburbs of Boston and Hartford, Connecticut, are an easy cougar's walk from the big woods of northern New England, which could support native cougars. If they do repopulate the forests of Vermont, New Hampshire, and Maine, or of New York State's Adirondacks, expect more tawny visitations to the big cities of the Northeast.

CHAPTER 2

COUGAR ATTACKS
AND HOW TO SURVIVE THEM

ven where cougars thrive, the chances of being attacked by one, much less killed, are minimal compared, say, to being the victim of a drunk driver. That said, if you or someone you love happens to be one of the unlucky people who falls victim to the very large, very sharp fangs and claws of a cougar, statistics are meaningless. Cougar researcher E. Lee Fitzhugh of the University of California at Davis put it well in a report on cougar attacks presented at a mountain lion workshop in 1996: "Something about even a small chance of being eaten by a large carnivore wrests the human imagination from the logic of numbers."

The increase in numbers, as opposed to the attacks in total, is starting to get scary. The evidence is clear that since the 1990s, attacks by cougars on humans have multiplied at an astonishing rate. Following the death of Iris Kenna in Cuyamaca Rancho State Park, California Fish and Game's Jeff Weir described the fatal attack as "a tragedy we're not sure we can prevent from happening again" (*Los Angeles Times,* December 13, 1994). He was right. Since then, cougars have killed several other people in California, and elsewhere as well. Although there are no definitive statistics on attacks, of the twenty known deaths by cougar since 1900, more than half have occurred since 1990. The same proportion holds for the approximately one hundred attacks, in total, during the same period.

Arguably the most comprehensive analysis of cougar attacks in the United States and Canada was compiled in 1991 by cougar expert Paul Beier of Northern Arizona University, president of the Society for Conservation Biology, a global community of conservation professionals. Beier noted even then that cougar attacks "have increased in the last two decades," citing as the most obvious and probable cause "the increased numbers of cougars and humans during that time."

Beier defined an attack "as an incident in which the cougar bit, clawed or knocked down a human." He excluded cases when cougars reacted after they were deliberately approached or provoked. Beier documented only fifty-three attacks in the century before 1991, a total lower than some other counts but nevertheless significant. Even so, it took only about a dozen years after that for the number to double, suggesting an almost exponential increase in cougar assaults.

Attacks are occurring in places where cougars and people have lived side by side amicably for years—suddenly and unexpectedly, in the fashion of *The Birds*. In January 2001, the province of Alberta experienced its first death by cougar ever, even though it has long had a substantial population of the animals. The victim was a thirty-year-old woman attacked while cross-country skiing in famed Banff National Park.

It stands to reason that examination of cougar attacks anywhere can provide know-how that helps insure the safety of people who live in cougar country—and those people are more numerous than ever, because cougar country now includes much more of the continent than it has for a century and a half or so.

The father of Frances Frost, the Banff National Park victim, admitted to the media that his own condo near the park had been built in what biologists call an ecological "corridor." An Edmonton lawyer, he blamed confrontations with cougars on humans encroaching into their territory, as he did when he built his home. His daughter, ironically, was an ardent environmentalist , as well as a dancer and writer, who had worked in the summer as an interpretive naturalist and, said her father, had great sympathy for the very species that killed her.

Ecological corridors provide pathways through which cougars and other creatures reach new territory within that crowded with humans. Corridors constitute an important element of wildlife ecology and are utilized in wildlife-management plans. Referred to as "lifelines for living," corridors link key areas of separated and fragmented wildlife habitat and ecosystems. Isolated wetlands, woodlands, prairies, and other habitats are even more functional when linked by corridors that funnel wildlife between them. One of the most important functions of corridors is that they prevent overpopulation and inbreeding. Corridors are conduits that channel animals from isolated populations to habitats that are the singles clubs of the animal world. In these places, animals from different gene pools can meet, mingle, and mate.

Among the most important corridors are riparian strips, such as woodlands along rivers and streams, often undeveloped because of wetlands. More than 70 percent of North American land-wildlife species use them, according to the U.S. Department of Agriculture. Slinking through the underbrush at the side of a major river, for example, a cougar can penetrate concrete-and-steel jungles almost as easily as it does natural forests.

Whether natural or created by humans, a corridor can be as immense as a mountain range or as restricted as a vegetation-covered highway median, even as small as a trickling, seasonal brook. Corridors can be impacted by a host of external factors, ranging from geological upheavals to construction of highways, and even human economics. When public works budgets shrink, wildlife often benefits, because grasses and shrubs on highway medians are not manicured, allowing for more food and cover. So, in one sense, an economic bust for humans can create boom times for wildlife. The present wildlife invasion of urban areas can be traced in part to the recession of the early 1980s, when scientists discovered that brush-choked highway medians were becoming significant highways of their own for wild animals.

Human impingement on corridors not only cuts off animal populations from one another and key habitat but can put people in the middle of dangerous traffic as animals channel through these conduits of nature. Game trails often follow corridors and, in a sense, create them. Often, humans follow the same routes when skiing or hiking. Cougars naturally frequent game trails, since the chances of making a kill are high there. Many years ago, I saw for myself the standard modus operandi used by the cougar when it attacks and kills large prey. The scene was not in a far wilderness but in my living room. It happened while I was a curator at the New York Zoological Society, with offices at the Bronx Zoo, and appearing as "The Animal Man" on *Patchwork Family,* a children's television show. One of the creatures I presented on camera was Carlos, a cougar kitten that had been taken from a private owner and given to the zoo for hand rearing. I took Carlos home so he could bond with me. My son, now a burly federal lawman, was a toddler at the time. He and the baby cougar, not much bigger than a housecat, engaged in bouts of play, chasing one another around the house and yard. During one such episode, Carlos jumped up on the living room couch and crouched there until my son toddled by. In a flash, Carlos leapt from the couch and pounced on his back, tumbling him to the floor. With tiny teeth fortunately not able to break the skin, the animal nipped my son at the back of his neck. My boy thought it was great fun, but I had witnessed a lethal behavior, the technique with which cougars ambush and kill prey, instilled by instinct even in a tiny kitten. Cougars typically attack from behind or above and kill by biting the back of the neck or head or suffocating the victim with a throat bite. Gruesome proof of the way the cougar targets the head area was provided in November 2013, when a cougar at an animal-rescue sanctuary in Portland, Oregon, turned on its female keeper and killed her. Dr. Christopher Young of the Oregon State Medical Examiner's Office said the victim had "devastating injuries in the critical areas of head and neck" (Associated Press, November 11, 2013).

The manner in which Iris Kenna was killed in Cuyamaca Rancho Park testifies to the tendency of cougars to spring upon prey from behind. The fangs of the cougar that killed her had penetrated the back of her neck and head. Authorities surmised she had tried to flee from the beast but that it ran her down and leapt upon her back. Attacking from the rear is a tendency shared by other large cats. Forest workers in the swampy Sunderbans of Bangladesh and India, a region notorious for maneating tigers, often wear masks with human faces on the back of their heads, to deter such surprise attacks. Studies show the technique works well.

Another deadly and tragic replay of what I saw in my living room happened in 1994, when a cougar attacked and killed a woman who was running on a trail in Auburn State Recreation Area, near a gated community forty miles north of Sacramento, California. The death of Barbara Schoener on April 23 had all the trademarks of a standard cougar attack. While the forty-year-old was jogging, a female cougar weighing about eighty pounds ambushed her. The cougar jumped Schoener from behind, perhaps from a ledge, as she jogged along the trail, and sank its fangs into the back of her neck and her skull, crushing the bone. When the cougar pounced, it knocked its victim down a steep slope alongside the trail. Investigators said Schoener, a strong marathoner,

120 pounds and almost six feet tall, apparently tried to fight off the animal. According to the sheriff's report, "Defensive wounds on Barbara's forearms and hands make it apparent she did struggle with the lion" (Associated Press, April 27, 1994).

At the time, apologists for cougars claimed the cat, which was lactating, was defending its young. Evidence showed, however, that the lion had selected Schoener as prey. The animal partly consumed her body, and then dragged it three hundred feet before caching it under sticks and leaves, typical of a cougar planning to return to its meal later.

If a cougar can kill an athletic adult in good shape, a child is obviously even more vulnerable. Parents who worry about cougars endangering their children should be aware of Paul Beier's 1991 study, which analyzed the key details of cougar attacks. Sixty-four percent of the victims in the attacks Beier studied were children, with those from five years to nine years of age the most vulnerable. Being in the company of other people, whether adults or other children, does not guarantee protection for a youngster, according to the study. Only 35 percent of the children attacked were alone. On the other hand, 43 percent of them were with other children when attacked and, surprisingly, 22 percent of child victims were with adults.

Beier's study was followed by the above-mentioned 1997 analysis by E. Lee Fitzhugh of human and cougar behavior during attacks. Fitzhugh went on to coauthor a paper in 2009 with UC Davis psychology professor Richard Coss, on a study of cougar attacks over a span of 110 years. The Coss-Fitzhugh research raises questions about how to avoid becoming cougar meat. Their study challenges the conventional wisdom of experts and wildlife agencies that running away from a cougar is almost always a mistake, and one that can have lethal consequences.

The standard advice is based on the fact that the attack response of cougars, like that of other cats, is triggered by a prey-sized object moving away from or across their position, especially if traveling at a good clip. Given this fact, one can understand why runners and joggers, like Barbara Schoener, are often attacked. Cross-country skiers fall into the same category. To a cougar's brain, their movement can resemble that of a fleeing deer or other prey and invites assault. A cougar can respond to such movement automatically, even if it is not hungry. One of my daughters lives in Marin County, California, near the Golden Gate Bridge and abutting a large nature reserve. She recounted an incident that seems to describe such an involuntary response. A friend was jogging along a path through the reserve when she glanced down and saw a cougar pacing along at her side. She screamed and, to her good fortune, the cat veered off into the woods and kept going. Apparently, it was not looking for food, even if its chase behavior had been activated. The screams broke its attention and defused the behavior.

In November 2011, a similar case occurred in Carson City, Nevada, when a jogger reported that a cougar had run parallel to him from a distance of about fifty yards before it broke off the chase. Other joggers have not been as fortunate. On January 14, 1991, an eighteen-year-old jogger near Idaho Springs, Colorado, was running alone on a remote trail near his high school. Scott Lancaster was jumped, killed, and partially consumed by a one-hundred-pound male lion.

Researcher Coss suggests, however, that turning one's back and running is not always an invitation to be victimized by a cougar. "Even though we found evidence that pumas will indeed chase, and capture, people who run," said Coss in a statement provided by the University of California at Davis on April 8, 2009, "running away might be the smartest move." Importantly, he qualified his statement with the following: "if you are in a situation that allows you to run in surefooted fashion and even strides—for a distance, on dry, flat ground rather than uneven terrain or deep snow."

Given that the terrain in which most cougar attacks occur is seldom as flat and open as a football field and that not all victims are in good enough shape to outrun a cat that can hit forty miles an hour in a short burst, the traditional wisdom remains a good bet in most situations: stand your ground, bluff, and if necessary fight like hell. Often, in fact, there is no other choice because, as researcher Fitzhugh noted in his 1997 report, cougars often blitz their victims without warning. Fitzhugh, assessing defensive choices when confronted by a cougar, evoked the folk story of a famous frontiersman using bluff to fight off a predator. "The showing of teeth, which people interpret as smiling, is often a threat display to the animal," he writes. "Thus, Davy Crockett truly may once have 'grinned down' a bear. We know of no research or observation that supports 'grinning down' any dangerous animal, but once a puma attack is imminent, the human victim needs all the threatening display he/she can muster. Grinning, or showing your teeth, won't hurt."

Bluffing plays on the way unfamiliar objects that loom over cats can intimidate them. Fighting back does work and has saved the lives of many a cougar attack victim. A classic case is when friends of mountain biker Anne Hjelle furiously pounded her attacker with sticks and rocks until it released its hold on her head. In 2007, a California woman grabbed a log and beat a cougar frantically when it pounced on her husband of fifty years and began to maul him. When that did not work, she snatched a ballpoint pen from his pocket and stabbed the animal in the eye, then resumed clubbing with the log. The beast finally let go of the man's head and retreated. Wildlife officials credited the woman with saving her husband's life. In a much-publicized case, a Texas man used a pocket knife to drive off a small cougar that attacked his six-year-old son at a campsite in Big Bend National Park in February 2012. The boy was treated for scrapes and puncture wounds at a hospital, and then released. Having a gun handy can really tip the odds against cougars, as in the case of a Fort Collins, Colorado, man who grabbed his gun and killed one when it attacked his dog outside his home in 2006.

Like leopards in the Old World, cougars relish dog flesh. While the cats will flee from a pack of tough and experienced cougar hounds, they view little Fluffy as scrumptious fast food. Walking a dog through the woods in cougar country is like ringing the dinner bell. Where cougars are abundant, even walking a pet near home can be hazardous. A cougar can snatch a dog from right under its owner's nose as fast as a frog takes a fly with its tongue. So discovered a woman who was walking her dachshund-Chihuahua mix, Buster, on a leash in Carmel Valley, California, during a night in early March, 2012. Shortly before midnight, Patty Small took Buster into her yard to heed nature's call. Buster was less than three feet away from her, leashed, when a cougar swooshed out of the dark, grabbed the pooch by the head, and disappeared with it into the night, trailing the leash. Small lost Buster, but the cougar's choice of prey was a stroke of luck for her.

Attacks that violate such intimate human space as a backyard raise fears that the weird aggressiveness displayed by the cougars of Cuyamaca Ranch Park is becoming more common. Wildlife agencies are wrestling with some tough questions in this respect, the answers to which are necessary in balancing the needs of both humans and cougars.

Are cougars really becoming bolder and losing their respect for humans, or is the increase in and brash nature of attacks simply a factor of there being more cougars and more people in the same places? Is it possible that cougars are losing their fear of people who are entering the wild armed with nothing more than a birder's guide, a hiking staff, and binoculars? Would it help to have more guns in the woods? Are cougars more likely to keep their distance in places where they are hunted?

Whatever the answers, you are statistically more likely to be attacked by a cougar than a decade ago, but why this is so is difficult to pin down. Admittedly, it is hard to argue with the assertion that more cougars coupled with more people increase the likelihood of attacks. As for taking the presence of people for granted, it does not seem to lessen the chance of attacks, noted Paul Beier in 1991, nor does hunting. Beier's study noted that twenty of the attacks he documented occurred on Canada's Vancouver Island. Then, as now, Vancouver Island is the cougar-attack capital, with more incidences there than anywhere else, although California competes for that dubious honor. Vancouver Island had a human population of about seven hundred thousand during the 1990s, increasing by more than one hundred thousand by the beginning of the twenty-first century. It has a hunting season for cougars and is a big-game hunting mecca. Unlike British Columbia, where Vancouver Island is located, California bans cougar hunting, although about eighty-five cats are killed annually by wildlife agents because they pose a danger to people and domestic animals. By way of comparison, South Dakota, with its population of a couple of hundred animals, allows about two dozen cougars to be killed by hunters annually.

By and large, people who live where cougars regularly appear are familiar enough with them to know what to do when confronted by one. People who are new to cougars or reside in places they are recolonizing do themselves a favor by heeding the Boy Scout motto and being prepared. Just in case. Cougar authority E. Lee Fitzhugh offered a summary of cougar predatory behavior—he used the name *puma*—at the cougar workshop in San Diego in 1996 (see Table 2.1). It includes appropriate human responses to various phases of this behavior.

Of course, a person attacked by a cougar has a better chance of surviving if outside help arrives during the assault. In March 2012, a California man claimed he was saved from a cougar attack by a most unlikely rescuer. While hiking in wild country, Robert Biggs spotted a mother black bear and cub by a stream. Suddenly, a cougar jumped him from behind, knocking him to his knees. According to Biggs, as he struck the cougar with a rock pick he carried for prospecting, the mother bear rushed over and grabbed the cougar by the neck. The two creatures battled for a few moments until the cougar cut and ran. Biggs figured that the cat was stalking the bear cub and that he'd walked into the line of fire.

One way or another, as cougars increase, so will interactions with people. Dr. Clay Nielsen, who led the research documenting the return of cougars to the prairie states and beyond, had this to say when discussing the future of cougars in areas that the cats have recolonized (Nielsen references the Midwest in this June 2012 press release announcing the study findings, but the observation applies anywhere there are people and cougars): "Much of the Midwest has lived without large carnivores such as cougars for more than 100 years. How will we all get along—or will we?"

The verdict remains out on that one.

Safety Tips: Cougars

Virtually all state and provincial wildlife agencies within established cougar country offer tips for surviving an encounter with a cougar and how to live with these animals as neighbors. Among the best are those of the Arizona Game and Fish Department and the British Columbia Ministry of Environment, found on their websites and adapted here.

Table 2.1 A Summary of Puma Predatory Behavior and Suggested Associated Human Response

Activity	Meaning	Human Risk
Puma far away and moving away	Secretive and avoidance	Insignificant
Puma more than 100 yards away, various positions and movements, attention directed away from people	Indifference	Slight, provided human response is appropriate
Puma more than 50 yards away; various body positions; ears up; may be changing positions; intent attention toward people; following behavior	Curiosity	Slight for adults given proper response. Serious for unaccompa children
Puma closer than 50 yards away; intense staring at humans; hiding	Assessing success of attack	Substantial
Intense staring and hiding coupled with crouching and/or creeping toward humans	Moving to attack position	Serious if within 200 yards
Crouching; tail twitching; intense staring at humans; ears erect; body low to ground; head may be up	Pre-attack; awaiting opportunity	Grave
Ears turned so the "fur" side is forward; tail twitching; body and head low to ground; rear legs may be "pumping" or "treading" gently up and down	Imminent attack; puma is ready to leap	Extreme

Source: E. Lee Fitzhugh, University of California, Davis, Department of Wildlife, Fish, and Conservation Biology

Keep children where they can be observed

Avoid rapid movements, running, loud, excited talk. Stay in groups; keep children with adults. Observe puma. For agencies, this may indicate future problems if repeated.

Hold small children; keep older children close to an adult. Do not turn your back on puma; assume standing position on ground, rocks, or large equipment that is above puma if possible. Look for sticks, rocks or other weapons and pick them up, using an aggressive posture while doing so. Watch puma at all times. However, if puma sits, looks away, and grooms itself, this is not a predatory situation and you should imitate the puma, but keep it in peripheral vision. For agencies, consider warning visitors and limiting hiking to groups.

All of the above steps, plus place older children behind adults. If a safer location or one above the puma is available, go there. Do not run. Raise hands and other objects such as jackets above head so as to present image of bulk as high as possible. Prepare to defend yourself.

Take all the above actions. If possible, move slowly to place large objects such as trees, boulders between yourself and the puma, but do not lose sight of the puma. Smile! (Show your teeth). Make menacing sounds; throw things if puma is close enough to hit.

Do all of the above and use whatever weapons you have. If you have lethal weapons take careful aim and use them now. Pepper spray may be effective if puma is close enough and downwind. If you have rocks or other items that can be thrown, do so.

Prepare to defend yourself in close combat. Fight back. Make menacing noises. The attack may happen within seconds. If you have any chance of averting it, it is by acting aggressively toward the puma. If the distance is too great to use a stick, run rapidly toward the puma until you can put the stick in its face and eyes. If you lack a stick, run toward the puma with arms high, making loud noises. Stop before you are within striking distance of its paws. Rapid movements towards the puma, especially from above it, may still deter an attack. Avoid positions below the puma; do not turn your back on it.

When in mountain lion country:

- Do not hike, jog, or ride your bicycle alone in mountain lion country: Go in groups, with adults supervising children.
- Keep children close to you: Observations of captured wild mountain lions reveal that the animals seem especially drawn to children. Keep children in your sight at all times.
- Do not approach a mountain lion: Most mountain lions will try to avoid a confrontation. Give them a way to escape.
- Do not run from a mountain lion: Running may stimulate a mountain lion's instinct to chase. Instead, stand and face the animal. Make eye contact. If there are small children there, pick them up if possible so they don't panic and run. Although it may be awkward, pick them up without bending over or turning away from the mountain lion.
- Do not crouch or bend over: A person squatting or bending over looks a lot like a four-legged prey animal. When in mountain lion country, avoid squatting, crouching, or bending over, even when picking up children.
- Appear larger: Raise your arms. Open your jacket if you are wearing one. Throw stones, branches, or whatever you can reach without crouching or turning your back. Wave your arms slowly and speak firmly in a loud voice. The idea is to convince the mountain lion that you are not prey and that you may be a danger to it.
- Fight back if attacked: Many potential victims have fought back successfully with rocks, sticks, caps, jackets, garden tools, and their bare hands. Since a mountain lion usually tries to bite the head or neck, try to remain standing and face the attacking animal.

If you live in mountain lion country:

- Don't feed wildlife: By feeding deer or other wildlife in your yard, you may inadvertently attract mountain lions, which prey upon them.
- Deer- and rabbit-proof your landscape: Avoid using plants that deer prefer to eat; if landscaping attracts deer, mountain lions may be close by.
- Landscape for safety: Remove dense and/or low-lying vegetation that provides good hiding places for mountain lions and coyotes, especially around children's play areas; make it difficult for wild predators to approach a yard unseen.
- Closely supervise children: Keep a close watch on children whenever they play outdoors. Make sure children are inside before dusk and not outside before dawn. Talk with children about mountain lions and teach them what to do if they encounter one.
- Install outdoor lighting: Keep the house perimeter well lit at night—especially along walkways—to keep any approaching mountain lions visible.
- Keep pets secure: Roaming pets are easy prey for hungry mountain lions and coyotes. Either bring pets inside or keep them in a kennel with a secure top.

CHAPTER 3

REAP WHAT YOU SOW:

*How the Environmental Movement
and Urban Sprawl Triggered
the Animal Invasion*

T he original 1984 *Red Dawn,* a film about a Soviet invasion of the United States, is one of my favorites. It pro-
pagandizes the right to bear arms under the Second
Amendment to the United States Constitution. While I tend
toward progressive on political, social, and economic issues, I
hold the Second Amendment sacrosanct. Perhaps I also like
the film because a little more than three decades before it
was produced, I experienced a *Red Dawn* of my own, if only
for a few moments.

At first I blinked my eyes in disbelief. But there they were.
Cresting the hills rimming the North End of Waterbury,
Connecticut, then famed as the Brass City, Russian bombers,
in perfect V formation, bore down upon my unsuspecting fellow townspeople. Only moments before, the horizon had been
clear as I surveyed it through binoculars, while on duty as
a thirteen-year-old member of the Ground Observer Corps.
An adjunct of the United States Air Force, the GOC, as it
was known, originated during World War II. It lasted into
the Cold War, when it numbered about 160,000 volunteers,
many of whom were housewives, seniors, and teenagers like
me. With the little pair of silvery metal GOC wings pinned
to my shirt, I took my weekly turn tracking air traffic from
station Bravo-Metro-Five-Three-Red, based in a dusty little
room within the white tower atop City Hall.

Back to the Russian planes. The aircraft I was watching had to be the enemy, because, based on my brief training, their unfamiliar configuration told me they were not our own. What else could they be but Russian? (Back in the early 1950s, we never called them "Soviets.") A scary thrill coursed through me as I focused my binoculars upon the aircraft leading the apex of the V. Chagrin replaced excitement when I realized the wings of the lead plane were flapping. The Russian air armada was a flight of Canada geese migrating south on that October day.

Embarrassment turned back to excitement again as it hit me that I was seeing real, live Canada geese. For me, it was a bird-watching milestone. If I had known about the birding tradition of keeping a life list of species sighted, I would have had an entry. Never before had I seen a single Canada goose, much less a migrating flock of close to a hundred.

Today, Canada geese seem as common as house sparrows. When I was a teenager, virtually the only Canada geese in Connecticut were migrants from the North, swiftly passing through like my Russian "aircraft." Migrants seldom stayed for long or in any numbers. The annual winter count of geese in the state by biologists generally numbered less than two hundred individuals. The multitudes of Canada geese that today throng in and around urban waters and greenswards are partly a product of the way these birds have adapted to environmental changes caused by humans. More importantly, after suffering at human hands, they have prospered according to human whim and manipulation.

Briefly, Canada geese were managed back into abundance by state and federal wildlife biologists after unrestricted market hunting decimated most of their populations by the beginning of the last century. Hunting restrictions and transplants of geese from populations that had survived the onslaught rebuilt their numbers and did so in spades. Geese are grazers, and the lawns of parks, golf courses, and soccer fields are for them an endless salad bar. Even better for the geese, in many cases they can feed at their leisure, free of predators that are rugged enough to tackle an adult Canada. Estimates of today's Canada populations range from four million to eight million individuals. Moreover, they have spread to Europe. Europeans will soon learn that fifty Canadas can deposit two and a half tons of poop in a year.

Geese are not among the wild creatures on which this book focuses. Still, their proliferation mirrors the way in which the species considered here are establishing themselves in human population centers. The large, sometimes dangerous creatures that are invading town and city are part of a broader biological context, a new wildlife community that has hitherto not existed in populous regions.

The reason for the growing interaction between wildlife and people might seem obvious: the urban sprawl that began in the 1950s. But urban sprawl is too simplistic an answer. The outward expansion of cities and suburbs, with hordes of humans swarming into the countryside, is certainly a big piece in the puzzle, but only one among many.

Urban sprawl did begin the process. If the boundaries of cities had remained static, the subject of this book would not exist. However, spread the cities did, like an amoeba engulfing and incorporating the countryside into itself.

Slightly more than 80 percent of the nation's people now reside in urban areas, according to figures released by the U.S. Census Bureau after the 2010 census. That percentage, however, can be misleading because of the nomenclature used by the bureau. It includes what the bureau defines as "urbanized areas," which have 50,000-plus inhabitants, and "urban clusters," which have a minimum population of 2,500 people. It is really a matter of population density. Population densities within urban areas range from almost 7,000 people per square mile to 363 people per square mile. Everything outside the urban categories is considered "rural."

Today, more residents of urbanized areas live in suburbs than in the core cities. As a working definition, moreover, the distinction between country, suburb, and city largely depends upon who makes it. Prior to 1972, when I lived in Fairfield County, Connecticut, if I heard someone talk about "the city," I knew they meant New York City. Where I have lived since, an hour's east of Fairfield County, "the city" often refers to New Haven. Likewise, I often hear Manhattanites describe the wealthy suburbs of Westchester County, New York, and Fairfield County as "the country." Compared to where I live, these areas are New York City beyond the Bronx.

Sprawl has undeniably brought people into contact with wildlife. Even so, it alone cannot account for the way in which animals from the wilds are penetrating the suburbs and reaching the heart of the biggest cities, such as New York City, Los Angeles, and Chicago. For sure, people are moving into wildlife country, but the traffic is two-way. Wilderness animals are filtering into human population centers from their remote natural strongholds, where their numbers have burgeoned. Cougar, coyote, and white-tailed deer are encountering people more frequently not just because, as Bambi's mother warned him in the classic Disney film, "Man is in the forest." It is also happening because Bambi is in the city.

A new relationship between people and wild animals has developed within the space of a single generation. When I was a boy, before suburban sprawl shifted into high gear, Connecticut had more open space than today, but the woodlands and fields were relatively silent and sterile, compared to the bustling wildlife now found there. The sight of a hawk in the sky was something to talk about for weeks afterward, if I could find someone among my boyhood crowd, besides my

best friend, John, who was as interested as I in nature. Deer? I saw my first one while driving through Pennsylvania while coming home from college in Indiana when I was nineteen years of age.

Now, it is an unusual day on which I do not see a deer, or at least the droppings and tracks that mark their passage. My town is halfway between Beantown and the Big Apple, a point where fans of the Yankees, Knicks, Giants, and Rangers merge—and wage verbal combat—with those of the Red Socks, Celtics, Patriots, and Bruins. When I arrived there in 1972, it was truly rural, although perhaps not according to the Census Bureau's definition. Today, with many of its new residents commuting to cities such as New Haven and Hartford, it is transitioning to suburban. By some measures, however, it remains rural. It contains vast blocks of state forest and watershed. Most residents—except, perhaps, newcomers from more developed communities—do not call the state troopers if they hear a gunshot. They know it is deer season, turkey season, or that a neighbor is defending the homestead's laying hens.

Less than two thousand people inhabited my town's thirty-five square miles when I moved in; its population has tripled but leveled off since. As the population density increased, so has the abundance and variety of wildlife. I see evidence of this virtually every day. Behind the desk at which I write is a wall of glass. It is a bank of windows that increases my fuel oil bill in winter due to heat loss but which I retain because it enables me to view a parade of wild creatures that visit my backyard and the mud puddle of a pond that lies there. The panorama that unfolds on a daily basis, in its own way, matches the wonders I have watched in places such as the Serengeti, the Andean altiplano, and the jungles of Southeast Asia. Otters, bobcats, mink, red foxes, the ubiquitous whitetail, a half-dozen species of hawks, egrets, and herons, wild turkeys, and coyotes all show up with a varying degree of regularity. A black bear has destroyed my gas grill, and as mentioned earlier, a cougar left its tracks in the snow over my garden.

A new ecology has evolved, in which multiple wild beasts live among dense concentrations of people in an environment created by planners, architects, contractors, carpenters, and highway workers, and sculpted by heavy equipment. More people live near wild animals than at any time in the history of the United States or, for that matter, North America. At first glance, the fact that wildlife thrives despite the disruption of nature by housing developments and the infrastructure that supports them seems a dichotomy. It is not.

The evolution of the backyard jungle begins in chaos as bulldozers wipe out woodland and meadow, and houses, shopping malls, and roads replace them. Undeniably, the expansion of city limits and the development of suburbs can destroy existing habitat and the animals that depend upon it.

After World War II, the first instant suburbs of cheek-by-jowl homes, such as the Levittowns of Long Island, New York, and Bucks County, Pennsylvania, were disasters as far as wildlife was concerned. As time passed, however, those first suburbs and the vegetation growing there matured. Due to increasing environmental awareness—and pressure upon developers—newer suburbs, often of less density than the first, left at least some room for nature.

If there is a plus side for nature when a suburb replaces forest or cornfield, it is that a suburb can have a greater variety of habitats than what went before it. Lawns and golf courses scattered among woodlands serve the same purpose as natural clearings. It creates what biologists call the "edge effect," meaning that when two habitats meet, biodiversity increases. The transitional zone between those habitats is called an ecotone; it has, in effect, a little of everything for the creatures adapted to habitats on either side. There, they can intermingle.

Ecotones created by suburbs constitute an ecology different from natural landscapes but not necessarily unfriendly to wildlife. These habitats created by humans have been particularly good to adaptable animals of medium size such as raccoons and opossums—and now, coyotes. Among large creatures, white-tailed deer, which find edges more to their liking, are now more numerous in some suburbs than in adjacent rural areas. Why this is not necessarily a good development for deer or people will be explained in the pages that follow. Deer also attract less benign animals, predators such as coyotes and cougars.

As cities and suburbs were growing, the environmental movement sprouted, emerging with full force after the first Earth Day, in 1970. Probably because so many environmental activists were themselves children of the city and its environs, the destruction of nature by rampant sprawl became

one of their primary concerns. Savvy wildlife biologists shopping around their research for funding during the 1970s knew that their chances increased if they could work an urban angle into their grant proposals. Improving aquatic habitats to promote urban fishing by inner-city residents was a popular theme, and still is. Conservation biology at the time stressed efforts aimed at improving the environmental health of cities and towns to make them more livable for wild creatures as well as humans. Conservation organizations—the National Wildlife Federation, for example—launched programs that helped homeowners improve their backyard-wildlife habitat.

Typical of the emphasis on urban wildlife was a symposium held in Springfield, Massachusetts, in November 1974. "Wildlife in an Urbanizing Environment" was sponsored by more than a half-dozen environmental agencies and organizations, including the U.S. Department of Agriculture, the Department of Forestry and Wildlife Management of the University of Massachusetts, and the Wildlife Society. The

symposium attracted such heavyweights of wildlife conservation as Durward L. Allen, wildlife ecology professor at Pur-
due University; Lynn A. Greenwalt, director of the U.S. Fish
and Wildlife Service; and Greenwalt's predessor at the service, John S. Gottschalk, who spearheaded the first federal
endangered-species act, the banning of DDT, and the comeback of the whooping crane.

Allen set the tone of the symposium, declaring that for
humans to survive and prosper, "Our management of wildlife
in the urban environment has a critical part to play." Par-
ticipants discussed ways to improve the lot of wildlife in an
urban environment and how to handle the reaction of people to wild-animal neighbors. For the most part, the neighbors under consideration were creatures like mallards and
raccoons. Back then, few biologists were planning for a time
when those neighbors would frequently include cougars and
moose. That said, the 1970s marked the first time that wildlife biologists began to extensively develop ways to manage
wildlife in urban environments. Researchers of the U.S. Forest Service, for instance, found that cemeteries contained 34
percent of the 4,903 acres of open space remaining in Boston
and nine immediate suburbs. Mount Auburn Cemetery in
Cambridge has become a famed birding spot, with tours going there, particularly during migrations.

Conservationists caught up in the environmental fer-
vor of the time literally rolled up their sleeves and jumped
into urban-wildlife projects. Executives of the Bronx Zoo left
their comfortable offices and waded into the putrid waters
of the polluted Bronx River to help New York City's parks
department and local conservationists start a cleanup of the
waterway, which is still ongoing. The program has been highly successful. Water that was noxious and filthy now supports
the first beavers to inhabit New York City in two centuries.

The purposeful wilding of cities continues. On May 7, 2006,

the *San Francisco Chronicle* oozed, "San Francisco is joining Seattle, New York, Miami and two dozen other metropolises in protecting nature in the city—slivers of marshes, grasslands, oak woodlands, dunes and rock outcrops that have looked mostly the same over the past 1,000 years." The article states that in these places, people could "walk in peace and observe nature." That is nicely warm and fuzzy, but San Francisco lies within country populated by creatures such as cougars and rattlesnakes that conceivably could hole up in these little enclaves of nature.

The success of wildlife in urban areas needs to be viewed in the context of the overall emphasis on wildlife conservation sparked by mounting environmental awareness on the part of science and society at large. Efforts to restore the health of rivers and to eliminate DDT and similar pesticides promoted biodiversity and enabled many species to recover. Wildlife in general benefited from species-recovery programs, wildlife habitat improvement, and better management techniques. Reintroduction and relocation of wildlife populations evoked a generally benevolent public attitude, except on the part of people such as the western ranchers who detest wolf reintroduction.

Meanwhile, since early in the last century, large portions of the nation, particularly in the eastern third, have reverted from cleared agricultural land to forest. Agriculture, particularly land devoted to a single crop, is utilized by far fewer species of wildlife than is natural cover. At the time of European contact, what became the United States had about a billion acres of forest, by far the greatest percentage east of the Mississippi River. Figures from the U.S. Forest Service reveal the extent of forest destruction caused first by agriculture and then by logging. By 1900, only 700 million acres remained. Since 1900, even though the nation's population has tripled, the nation's forests have remained relatively stable, according to the Forest Service. Actually, it has increased slightly, peaking at 745 million acres, more than half of it in the East.

The rosy outlook may be deceiving. The Forest Service maintains that while forests in the interior of the country have been stable or increased, those on both coasts have suffered losses. Regionally, forces such as urbanization and mining have caused forest losses, according to a study published in the journal *BioScience* in 2010 by Mark Drummond, a U.S. Geological Survey geographer. Between 1972 and 2006, urbanization and other development took 10 percent of Rhode Island's forestland.

Regional trends aside, the United States has trees aplenty. Some cities have so many trees that "urban forest" is almost a biome of its own. About 3.6 million trees grow within the limits of Chicago, for example. A count by the New York City Parks Department released on Arbor Day 2007 reported 592,130 trees growing on streets alone.

One of the great forests of the world lies in Central Africa. Looking down upon it from the window of a jetliner crossing the midsection of the continent, one sees a vast expanse of green, horizon to horizon. Many times I have flown on commercial aircraft over the Connecticut countryside in which I live, and a handful of times in single-engine planes. In season, the greenery below evokes images of the African rainforest. A few buildings peep through the woodland canopy, but if I were unfamiliar with the territory, I might think of it as wilderness. During the winter, the true nature of the landscape is revealed. All those leaves hide towns, streets, homes, commercial buildings, and substantial numbers of people. Nevertheless, forest is intermingled with housing, and commercial development is more than enough to support a thriving variety of wildlife.

Of all states, Connecticut has the highest proportion

of land—72 percent—classified as wildland-urban interface (WUI), a designation used by natural-resource professionals and federal and state agencies that deal with wildfires. WUI describes where development pushes against or is interspersed with wildland vegetation. Connecticut's 3.5 million people live in a state 60 percent forested. By contrast, New Mexico's WUI percentage is 1.6, according to a study by the U.S. Forest Service and University of Florida.

WUI has several versions. One is the classic interface of urban sprawl shoving against natural areas, creating a distinct frontier. Another is a mixture of natural areas and urban land uses, much like that where I live. Another version is the isolated interface, such as where vacation-home communities are plunked down in the wilderness. Yet another is interface islands, chunks of undeveloped land, often riverine corridors, left over amid urban sprawl.

While most residents of the United States live in land designated as urban, the major portion of the nation's land, by far, lies outside urban boundaries in what the Census Bureau designates as "rural." By no means is all of it wilderness, but an increasing amount qualifies as such. A major force for preserving wild country has been the federal Wilderness Act. By its half-century anniversary, in 2014, it had enabled the protection of more than 109 billion acres of wild country as official wilderness.

Given sufficient habitat, biologists can target imperiled species for management and restoration. Such efforts enabled many depleted creatures, such as American alligators and cougars, to recover and thrive in the land beyond the city. During the 1960s, alligators were declared an endangered species, due partly to habitat loss but mainly because poachers massacred them for their hides. Enforcement of anti-poaching laws and protection of habitat allowed the alligator to recover and then proliferate. To people living near alligators, they have gone from novelty to pest to menace.

The fall and rise of creatures such as alligators and white-tailed deer exemplifies the profundity of human impact upon wildlife. Humans caused the fall of these species, then manipulated them back into abundance, even overabundance. Importantly, it should be pointed out, nature also lent a hand. The ability to adapt to changing demands on living and the overall resiliency of nature cannot be overstated.

Resurgence of the alligator also shows how protection can result in too much of a good thing. Especially in a time when many wild areas are fragmented, a species can saturate its habitat and exceed its maximum carrying capacity. At that point, there is no choice for wildlife. It is either move out or starve. Natural corridors that enable movement are recovering after suffering losses due to forces such as large-scale farming, stream channelization, and suburban planning that made no provisions for nature. With the passage of time, many corridors, especially those that are artificial, have matured ecologically, adding to their vegetative cover and thus their value. Some state and federal wildlife agencies are creating artificial corridors where natural channels are nonexistent but needed. When the North Carolina Department of Transportation decided in 2012 to widen U.S. Route 64 from two to four lanes across the Alligator River National Wildlife Refuge, research began into the problem of the region's plentiful black bears crossing the highway. Besides bears, the area is populated by reintroduced and endangered red wolves. Researchers developed a plan for underpasses suitable for both species to let them cross safely.

Not surprisingly, as corridors have improved traffic has increased on these highways for wildlife. The so-called Milford mountain lion was killed by a vehicle along the Wilbur Cross Parkway, which, with the connected Merritt Parkway, were planned as scenic, heavily planted roadways, opened in the 1930s and 1940s. The margins and medians of these parkways form a corridor of trees, grassy spaces, and brush through some of the most heavily populated areas of New England. Following the parkway, the cougar had slipped unnoticed into the heart of suburbia. Granted, I exaggerate, but when I think of wilderness lands producing creatures that penetrate the megalopolis I am reminded of science fiction films depicting postapocalypse "bubble cities," walled off from vast wastelands populated by zombies. The zombies are now breaching the bubble.

The breaching of urban perimeters by large wild creatures is not an anomaly, nor is it unique to North America. It is a growing trend, a phenomenon that has never happened before, and which is evidenced in many parts of the world. In November 2006, *Science,* the prestigious journal of the American Association for the Advancement of Science, ran a report called "The Carnivore Comeback." It described how European carnivores—bears, wolves, wolverines, and lynx, are increasing in numbers and expanding into areas where they have been extinct for centuries. As in North America, pressure from conservationists during the 1960s and 1970s resulted in efforts to save dwindling European species and habitat. Species prospered and began to move around. Just like on this side of the Atlantic, reintroduction of species by wildlife agencies further increased animal numbers. Brown bears from Slovenia have been transplanted to the Pyrenees to bolster the dwindling population there. Shepherds and farmers of the region are furious, much like ranchers in the western United States who are up in arms, sometimes literally, over wolf reintroduction.

Many of the former Eastern Bloc countries contain large tracts of wilderness, as wild and woolly as the Canadian Rockies or the big woods of Maine. Since borders have opened, these areas are the source of wolves and bears that

are moving west as well as north into Scandinavia. Wolves, in particular, are howling again in parts of the former East Germany that have lost human population due to a poor economy.

Wild boars are a continent-wide problem but especially in France, where their numbers have doubled to a million in a decade. The huge wild pigs destroy field and forest, cause traffic accidents, kill small animals, ravage crops, and sometimes injure, and even kill, humans. Boars thrive on corn, more of which is being grown for biofuel, so their food supply is more bountiful than ever. Warmer winters brought by climate change have also boosted the boar's key wild-food supply: acorns and chestnuts. Mild winters result in another benefit to boars. Fewer young and aging animals fall victim to harsh weather. France and other European countries are desperately trying to rekindle interest in hunting to cut down boar numbers.

Japan, where an ancient hunting tradition is viewed with contemporary distaste, is now wondering whether to buck public sentiment and encourage sportsmen to take to the field. The reason: like many American suburbs, parts of Japan have a serious deer problem, although with a different species, the sika. Japan's deer population has been doubling every four years and now approaches a million animals. A population of more than one hundred thousand deer on the main Japanese island of Honshu—where Tokyo is situated—is gobbling up so much produce and landscape plantings that some groups are calling for a truly drastic measure, reintroduction of the wolf, in this case from abroad. Wolves went extinct in Japan at the beginning of the twentieth century due to overhunting of the deer on which they fed and of wolves themselves.

A more likely measure would be to bring in other hunters from abroad, in the person of wealthy foreign sportsmen. It might be necessary, if hunting is employed as a management tool, because it is easier for the average Japanese citizen to obtain licenses for firearms and hunting on Mars than in his or her own country. By using foreigners to hunt, the government would keep firearms out of Japanese hands.

On the Asian mainland, the Chinese are suffering the impact of a government ban on bear hunting. Asian black bears, more feisty than the North American black bear, have been invading villages in the province of Yunnan. The bear population has outgrown its natural food supply and has been raiding crops.

Nepal has received kudos from conservationists for preserving habitat within magnificent national parks and successfully protecting endangered species. It came as a shock to many wildlife protectionists when the country's government announced in 2013 that it will take steps to cap the growth of wildlife populations. The announcement came after a public outcry over depredations by creatures such as tigers, rhinos, elephants, and leopards. Wild animals emerging from parks into nearby settlements are killing several dozen Nepalese a year.

"Move Over Squirrels: Leopards Are the New Backyard Wildlife," headlined a March 28, 2013, press release promoting a study in India by the New York City–based Wildlife Conservation Society. In terms of adaptation to a wide variety of habitats and vastness of range, the leopard rivals the New World's cougar. While they have vanished from much of their range, leopards are very much in evidence where they have survived. Although stealthy, they are not deterred by human presence. I once visited a house near Kenya's Nairobi National Park where, almost every night, a leopard appeared and climbed atop a carport roof. From its perch, it surveyed the neighborhood, as leopards are wont to do while seated upon outcroppings of rock called kopjes.

Worldwide, it seems, the place where the wild things are is in the backyard; the front yard, too. A Norwegian scientist quoted in the 2007 article "The Carnivore Comeback," mentioned earlier, summed up the current state of affairs when he noted that people will now have to reconcile themselves with the fact that they are sharing space with large wild creatures: "Wolves and bears are part of the 21st century landscape."

CHAPTER 4

COYOTE ON THE CUL-DE-SAC:
Coyotes in Cities and New Wolves in the Woods

"Not dogs, wolves." That was the gist of what Canadian wolf expert Douglas Pimlott told me back in the 1970s when I asked him about the "coydogs," supposed coyote-dog hybrids that were chasing deer around the New England woods. Despite Pimlott's world-class reputation as a scientist, and his status as a father of Canada's environmental movement, many of his colleagues disagreed with his opinion that big, aggressive coyotes colonizing the Northeast were part wolf, not coyote-dog mixes as most everyone else claimed.

Had he not passed away in 1978, Pimlott probably would be enjoying a prolonged "I told you so" moment. Genetic studies of eastern coyotes reported in 2009, 2010, and 2011 indicate that, even though some of them may have a smattering of dog genes, the so-called eastern coyote does indeed possess wolf genes and has morphed into the coywolf. The name may sound a bit hokey, but it has gained acceptance among biologists.

Four of these biologists are Jonathan G. Way, of Eastern Coyote Research in Massachusetts, and Linda Rutledge, Tyler Wheeldon, and Bradley N. White of Ontario's Trent University. Describing their findings, they stated, "the eastern Coyote should more appropriately be termed 'Coywolf' to reflect their hybrid . . . origin." Indeed, the coywolf has been

73

granted the imprimatur, for what it is worth, of an entry in *Wikipedia.* Just as Pimlott told me, coyotes interbred with wolves while passing through the region north of the Great Lakes as they expanded their range from the West. They carried lupine genes, and consequent increasing body size, with them on a migration that ended on the Eastern Seaboard. Some scientists even suggest they constitute a new species of canid in the making, an example of evolution in action.

As described later in this chapter, the genetic mix that produced the coywolf is a little more complicated than Pimlott first described to me. Evolving species or hybrid, however, for all practical purposes there is a new wolf in the woods of the Northeast and it is showing up not only in forest and field but in the backyards of soccer moms and in big-city parks from Virginia to the Canadian Maritime Provinces. Once surreal, the sound of coywolves, howling like hellhounds as they gather for the hunt within shotgun range of my doorstep, is now routine. The vocalizations of the coyote, by the way, gave rise to its name, from the Aztec word *coyotl,* meaning "barking dog." Those barks now echo far and away from the western grasslands and deserts that are the coyote's original range. Including coywolves, coyotes have expanded their turf to all compass points and now prowl every state except Hawaii. South of the border, they have pushed out of Mexico and penetrated as far as the Panama Canal. All told, they have doubled their range since the days of the Last Frontier.

Within that vast area they seem at least as comfortable in suburbs and cities as in the countryside. Like United States Marine Corps Force Reconnaissance and Army Pathfinders, coyotes were the advance wave of carnivores that paved the way for larger species to invade the city. Coyotes have long been part of the wildlife scene within the municipal limits of

Los Angeles and other western cities. Along with the occasional cougar, they invade the city through brush-filled canyons and other corridors. Packs of them roam L.A.'s Griffith Park. Coyotes in Griffith Park may not seem surprising, but Central Park in Manhattan? Indeed, coyotes now can be considered Manhattanites. During February 2010, they were seen in New York City's Morningside Heights, near Columbia University, and in Midtown, within Central Park no less. The discovery of coyotes in New York City's most famous, and at times infamous, park naturally prompted quips about predators on four legs as well as two prowling there after dark. The outer boroughs of the city have even more coyotes, especially Staten Island, which still has a few farms and a sizable white-tailed deer herd. The vast—two thousand acres—Rock Creek Park, in northeastern Washington, D.C., also has a deer herd and, not unexpectedly, coyotes, which arrived there in 2004. During the early 1990s, nuisance coyotes removed from Chicago neighborhoods typically numbered less than twenty individuals a year. Before the decade was over, the number approached four hundred. Stanley Gehrt, an expert on urban coyotes, wonderfully summed up how the coyote has made it in the city in a 2010 book he coedited, *Urban Carnivores:* "The icon of wilderness has quickly become a denizen of the city."

The total number of coyotes inhabiting their immense range is virtually incalculable. Arizona alone has an estimated two hundred thousand coyotes, even though hunters kill between twenty thousand and thirty thousand of them each year. During the summer, before winter takes its toll, New York State has between twenty thousand and thirty thousand, while Maine has a similar number.

From the tropics to the Arctic fringes, coyotes *(Canis latrans)* differ sufficiently to the scientist that taxonomists generally distinguish nineteen different subspecies. Most are sufficiently alike that they look the same to the untrained eye, although the size of the eastern coyote, or coywolf, sets it apart from the rest. In terms of bulk, the coywolf is a throwback to the Pleistocene, when Ice Age versions of animals such as coyotes and bison were much larger than their counterparts today. Research by scientists of the National Evolutionary Synthesis Center in Durham, North Carolina, determined that Pleistocene coyotes overlapped in size with wolves.

Published in the *Proceedings of the National Academy of Sciences* in 2012, the research suggested that at the end of the Pleistocene, from 11,500 to 10,000 years ago, coyotes shrank to the size found in most subspecies today. Downsizing took place in what is "a mere blink of the eye in geological terms," according to the authors. Disappearance of hulking coyotes and the survival of smaller, quicker individuals seems related to the extinction of many large North American animals during the same period. Size was no longer an advantage in securing prey. Agility and stealth were needed to catch the quick little creatures that remained, so selection, in turn, favored the lightweight coyotes. In turn, carrying fewer pounds meant coyotes could get by with less bulk in their diet, enabling them to survive on smaller meals.

The typical coyote of its original western range represents the root stock of all modern varieties and is pretty much the coyote that existed after the Pleistocene ended. The western coyote is primarily—but not exclusively—a creature of plains and deserts. It is a medium-sized creature, which reaches four to five feet long from nose to tail tip. Adults weigh from twenty to thirty-five pounds, with males larger than their mates. The upper coat is usually various shades of buff or gray, while fur covering the throat and belly is often white to cream color. The coyote's ears are pointed and erect, and when it runs, it carries its tail below the level of its back, not horizontally like a wolf. Coyotes can often live six to eight years in the wild. Mortality rates can be high, even without human hunting pressure. More than half of all juvenile coyotes die before adulthood.

The coyote's ability as a survival expert manifests itself when a population is severely depleted. Females begin breeding at an earlier age, and have larger litters than the normal four to five pups. The pups are born in dens, which the adults usually dig themselves, although they will take over abandoned holes of other animals and even space under buildings. Breeding season, when coyotes are most evident, generally spans the winter, with pups born two months after conception.

Coyote cubs are precocious, weaned in a month and then fed food regurgitated until they can hunt with the parents. As fall approaches, when they are ten weeks old at most, the pups depart their parents, disperse, and establish their own home ranges. A coyote's home territory is extremely variable and largely determined by the abundance of prey. Home ranges in desert and forested areas can exceed fifty square miles. Home territory in habitats with a patchwork of ecotones, and thus with plenty of edge to exploit, can be just a few square miles. Just as people living in the city can walk to the deli, pharmacy, and package store while country folk usually must drive, coyote home ranges are often relatively tiny in urban areas. For coyotes, a suburb, with its cats, rats, and garbage, is a big-box supermarket with one-stop shopping.

The adaptability of a coyote to so many different surroundings also stems from the fact that it is a very opportunistic feeder. A look at the list of foods it consumes suggests that there is not much a coyote will not eat, especially in the absence of its favorite fare, small rodents and rabbits. Lacking such, it does very well on carrion, insects, fruits, melons, berries, birds, frogs, snakes, plants, and seeds. Because coyotes are so opportunistic, garbage and pet meals left out-side homes furnish them with what is, in effect, fast food, and is part of the reason they thrive around people. In many parts of the West, coyotes also prey on sheep, goats, calves, and poultry, behavior that has led to their classification as ver-min and targeting by ranchers and farmers. Over the years, millions of coyotes have been killed by predator-control pro-grams waged by some states and the U.S. Department of Ag-riculture. That they still prosper is proof that they are evolu-tionary survival experts of the first order.

The extermination of the wolf over almost all its range below the Canadian border opened the door to a vast new home for the coyote. A study by the Wildlife Conservation Society, published in 2007, showed that coyote densities can be 30 percent lower in areas they share with wolves. European settlers of the United States brought their ancient antipathy for wolves with them, and the creatures were swept away as a result of manifest destiny. Into the vacuum strolled the coyote. Coyote expansion started about a century ago. Without wolves to kill them, as sometimes happens, and to lock up the food supply, coyotes moved from western plains and deserts throughout North America, from Alaska to Mexico. Exploiting changes wrought by people, they changed lifestyle, habitat, and food choices as need be. Just as they evolved smaller stature in a geological instant at the Pleistocene's end, so, in just a hundred years or so, modern coyotes have demonstrated that they are still evolutionary quick-change artists.

Ironically, despite the evil that wolves do to coyotes, the two have their own version of a love-hate relationship that enabled the interbreeding described to me by Douglas Pim-lott. A study under Dr. Roland Kays of the New York State Museum in Albany finally provided genetic evidence to sup-port the hybridization supposition. Published in the journal

Biology Letters during 2009, it sparked headlines about the "coyote in wolf's clothing." The authors summed up their findings in the abstract of their paper: "We suggest that hybridizaton with wolves in Canada introduced adaptive variation that contributed to larger size, which in turn allowed eastern coyotes to better hunt deer, allowing a more rapid colonization of new areas than coyotes without introduced wolf genes . . . enabling northeastern coyotes to occupy a portion of the niche left vacant by wolves."

Out of all the hoopla, the coywolf was born. The wolf may be the coyote's enemy and competitor but its genes also produced a supercoyote, if you will. What you have with the coywolf is a creature that is as adaptable and clever as a coyote while being as big and bad as a wolf.

The wolf that Kays cited as mating with coyotes is the Great Lakes wolf, which according to traditional taxonomy is a subspecies of *Canis lupus* that inhabits northern Minnesota and Wisconsin, Michigan's Upper Peninsula, and Canadian territory to the north. As mixing occurred to the north, coyotes were also migrating east on a route south of the lakes into Ohio, where they remained pretty much the pure coyote strain. The northern and southern migrants met up again when some of the incipient coywolves rejoined the pure strain in western New York and Pennsylvania. Researchers from the Smithsonian Institution, publishing in the *Journal of Mammalogy* during 2011, traced coyotes in Virginia and Rock Creek Park to animals produced by the convergence, to which wolf genes had been transferred. Meanwhile, other hybrids continued along a more northerly route toward New England. These coywolves of the Northeast appear to be the largest and most wolf-like of all.

With some individuals the size of a German shepherd dog, eastern coyotes can be twice as large as their western counterparts. Their skulls are wider and more robust, and their jaws are larger and designed for killing and eating animals the size of deer, rather than catching creatures like kangaroo rats that are coyote staples in the West. Scientists who study the morphology of canids opine that the changes in jaw structure and musculature are not the product of superfast evolution in migrating western-type coyotes, but are fashioned by wolf genes mingling with those of the coyote. Coywolves usually pursue deer in packs, like wolves, whereas western coyotes usually hunt individually or in twos and threes like, well, coyotes. The skeletal evidence supports the link with the wolf suggested by genetics research.

What DNA researchers proved at the genetic level has been evident to knowledgeable northeastern outdoorspeople for years. It does not take an expert to recognize that, whatever one wishes to call it, this new addition to the fauna of the Northeast acts a lot like a wolf. Not long after I talked with Pimlott, a friend of mine was chased by a pack as he rode his horse through our local state forest. He was not sure whether they were after the horse or him, and fortunately never found out, since he outdistanced them even though they can run at thirty miles per hour. Coyotes do not usually chase horsemen. For my money, if it looks like a wolf and acts like a wolf, it should be viewed as a wolf and treated as such.

As if to put a bloody exclamation point on the scientific research that identified coywolves, during the year that Dr. Kay's study was published, 2009, two, perhaps three of them, attacked and killed a nineteen-year-old female Canadian folk singer on a heavily traveled trail through Nova Scotia's Cape Breton Highlands National Park. Taylor Mitchell's career as a folk singer was taking off, big-time. She had just released her first album, been invited to perform at the Winnipeg Folk Festival, and was nominated for a Canadian Folk Music Award as Young Performer of the Year. A few days after the nomination, she was dead, savaged by coywolves in an attack that made international headlines and was the subject of an hour-long show on the National Geographic Channel. A near-dead Mitchell was found on the ground by two hikers who scared off the coywolves. It was, scientists said, not a defensive attack or a freak incident but a deliberate act of predation. A year later, a coyote bit the head of a sixteen-year-old girl sleeping at a campground in the same park. Coyotes usually don't attack fully grown adults, either. Bear in mind that the animals involved in both attacks had wolf genes just like those inhabiting Rock Creek and Central Parks.

To credit just the wolf with facilitating the boom times experienced by the coyote is probably oversimplifying the matter. It may be more precise to use the term *wolves*. Since about the beginning of the century, scientists have produced a flood of scientific research into the taxonomy of North American canids that has scrambled traditional views of not only what constitutes a coyote but also a wolf. Postulations based on this research about relationships between different groups of wolves and coyotes—particularly coywolves—have sparked debate among wildlife biologists and taxonomists that promises to continue for a long time to come. With some of the top minds in the world of wildlife sciences stirring the pot of argumentation, trying to fathom the proposed new order of things can leave the rest of us scratching our heads.

Suffice to say that when the results of the various studies are compared it is easy to surmise that there may be more varieties of North American canids than previously believed. Moreover, these creatures may be swapping genes promiscuously, producing hybrids like the coywolf and who knows what else in the future. It is a far cry from the traditional view that there were three species of wild canids on the continent: between eight and a couple of dozen subspecies of the gray, or timber, wolf *(Canis lupus);* the coyote; and the rather mysterious red wolf *(Canis rufus),* which was variously believed to be a subspecies of the gray wolf, a gray wolf–coyote hybrid, or a species on its own but with an ancestor shared by coyotes. Once common in the Middle Atlantic and southeastern regions of the country, it vanished from the wild but has been reintroduced in North Carolina. The traditional arrangement held fast until scientists began probing the intricacies of canid DNA. Genetic research has blurred the old view, and new studies may seem to make the situation even more cloudy rather than clarify it.

The picture began to get hazy when a change was made in the status of the eastern wolf, which has a core population in the Algonquin Provincial Park of Ontario and had an original range northeast and east of the Great Lakes. Until recently, it was considered a subspecies of the gray wolf called *Canis lupus lycaon*. Named after a king in Greek legend who was turned into a wolf by the capricious god Zeus, *lycaon* has been elevated by most biologists to a species in its own right, a designation that has been accepted by the U.S. Fish and Wildlife Service when it considers the conservation status of wolves. Research led by Dr. Robert Wayne of UCLA, published in the journal *Genome Research* under lead author Bridgett Von Holt in 2011, viewed the eastern wolf in an even newer light. It contends that the eastern wolf is genetically only slightly more wolf than coyote. Beyond that, according to the research, unlike the pure wolves farther west, Great Lakes wolves are 15 percent coyote. And the red wolf, the study results contend, is almost three-quarters coyote. Wayne's study also reexamined the genetics of the Northeastern coyote/coywolf, suggesting it was 9 percent dog and 9 percent wolf, the rest of its heritage being coyote.

The year after Wayne's study was published, a survey by Steven Chambers, a biologist for the U.S. Fish and Wildlife Service, showed how many different interpretations could be made of the various genetic studies. Eastern wolves, the survey noted, mate with both gray wolves and coyotes. Great Lakes wolves, according to Chambers's work, appear to be a mix of gray wolves and eastern wolves. Meanwhile, several Canadian researchers including Christoper Kyle and Paul Wilson contend that eastern wolves and red wolves are virtually the same, and moreover, descended from the same primitive ancestor as coyotes. Coywolves, according to this line of research, carry not genes of Great Lakes wolves but of eastern wolves that have recrossed with their close relative. Complicating the issue is an opinion voiced in the Associated Press by a U.S. Geological Survey scientist who is arguably the dean of modern wolf researchers. In May 2011, L. David Mech questioned that not enough genetic data were collected and analyzed to conclude the eastern wolf is a hybrid. Doubt voiced by a scientist who has been considered a top expert on wolves for decades casts a big shadow. Suffice to say that the conclusions reached so far based on genetic research into canid relationships cannot be etched in stone.

When one tries to compare the multiple opinions and studies, one reasonable conclusion at this point is that a whole bunch of wolf and coyote DNA has been thrown into a genetic mixer that has produced several types of canids of both wolf and coyote heritage, differing in how much of each. Researchers Jonathan Way and colleagues put it aptly in their paper on eastern wolf-coyote hybridization, published in 2010 in *Northeastern Naturalist: "Canis* soup." One way or the other, the delineation between coyotes and wolves as species seems to be in flux, especially in the region from the Great Lakes to the Atlantic Seaboard.

For almost all of my professional life, I have been a friend of a man who is one of those unusual individuals adept at several seemingly unrelated sciences and a well-published author of fiction as well as nonfiction. We met while we were both curatorial-level staffers at the New York Zoological

Society. Stephen Spotte, an iconoclastic product of West Virginia coal country, made his mark by running major public aquariums and in marine research. He remains an adjunct scientist at Mote Marine Laboratory, in Sarasota, Florida. The injection of Spotte here may seem intrusive, a digression from the subject of coyotes. Not so. In typical no-holds-barred fashion, Spotte has encapsulated what I believe is the best-informed opinion on the status of the entire coyote-wolf interbreeding debate. Early on in his 2012 book, *Societies of Wolves and Free-Ranging Dogs,* he states, "I doubt whether any admixed canid can properly be labeled a species, the obvious gradiation in geonomic composition making even the use of 'coyote' and 'wolf' problematical."

The blurring of taxonomic lines between coyotes and wolves is supported by a scientific paper published in October 2013 in the *Canadian Journal of Zoology.* The researchers were Dr. John Benson of Trent University and Dr. Brent Patterson of the Ontario Ministry of Natural Resources. They found that what they called eastern coyotes and hybrids of eastern coyotes and eastern wolves were taking down adult moose in Ontario. The prevailing wisdom has been that bringing down such a behemoth as a full-grown moose was beyond the physical capabilities of a coyote or coyote-like canid. Apparently, that idea has been trashed. The lighter canids could travel over snow in which moose mired down.

While coyotes in the Northeast were receiving the bulk of scientific attention and publicity ink, another batch of coyotes was quietly occupying a much larger section of the country. The old standby coyotes, minus the glamour of wolf lineage, were invading all of the Midwest and the South. The success of the creatures in and around Chicago led to an ongoing, multiyear study of urban coyotes that is becoming a prototype for the study of urban carnivores. When it was begun in 2000, the study was only supposed to last a year.

Chosen to conduct the study was Stanley Gehrt, the assistant professor of environmental and natural resources at Ohio State University who was then a research biologist for the Max McGraw Wildlife Foundation in Dundee, Illinois. During the 1990s, people in the Chicago metropolitan region began to flood the foundation with complaints about coyotes snagging their pets and even stalking their children. Meanwhile, the animal-control agency of Cook County, where Chicago is located, asked Gehrt to begin gathering information about the coyotes that the agency knew had taken up residence in and around the city. What the agency did not know was the extent to which the animals had colonized the area. The researchers had expected to find a few small coyote packs here and there throughout the city, with total population numbers in the range of several dozen, but the animals were ubiquitous, seemingly in every urban nook and cranny.

"Nine million people live in the greater Chicago area," Gehrt commented in a January 2005 research-news story on Ohio State's website. "We didn't think very many coyotes could thrive in such a highly urbanized area. We also thought that the few animals that were causing problems were probably used to living around people." The researchers never expected to find a couple of thousand coyotes, which turned out to be a reasonable estimate. "We couldn't find an area in Chicago where there weren't coyotes," Gehrt said. "They've learned to exploit all parts of their landscape." Some of the animals live in city parks, while others live among apartment and commercial buildings and in industrial parks. While parks and forest preserves enhance habitat for coyotes, Gehrt has discovered that coyotes do not need them but can stake out even residential areas as territories. Individual coyotes can live just about anywhere. Within the city, they retain their social structure. With their only real predator being the motor vehicle, coyotes tend to live longer in the city in general, while the chances of urban coyote pups surviving are five times that of their counterparts in the boonies.

Much of what Gehrt has learned comes from electronically tracking coyotes that have been captured and fitted with radio transmitters on collars. While Gehrt's coyote research is concentrated in Chicago , the results apply to most major metropolitan areas in North America. Since the study began, Gehrt and his colleagues have found that urban coyote populations are much larger than expected; that they live longer than their rural cousins in these environments; and that they are more active at nighttime than coyotes living in rural areas. "A coyote may eat the food that's left outside for a pet," Gehrt commented in the Ohio State news piece. "It's not uncommon to see a coyote pass through an urban or suburban neighborhood. But most coyotes aren't thrilled about being seen by people. Urban coyotes are more active at night than their rural counterparts, so humans don't see a lot of their activity. In many cases, coyotes are probably doing us favors that we don't realize—they eat a lot of rodents and other animals that people don't want around." Another plus for having coyotes in the neighborhood, according to Gehrt's study, is that they control Canada geese numbers by eating eggs in the nest.

As published in the Ohio State news story, Gehrt's findings also include:

> • *The prevalence of large packs. Coyotes prefer to hunt alone, but often form packs to defend territories. Gehrt estimates that roughly half of all urban coyotes live in territorial packs that consist of five to six adults and their pups that were born that year. These urban packs establish territories of about five to 10 square miles—a fraction of the area that a rural coyote pack would cover. Consequently, the population densities in the*

urban area are usually three to six times higher than rural populations.

Those urban coyotes that don't hunt in packs can cover ranges of 50 square miles or more, often in just one night. . . .

- *Urban coyotes survive far longer than their rural cousins. A coyote living in urban Chicago has a 60 percent chance of surviving for one year, while a rural coyote has a 30 percent chance of living for another year.*
- *Most coyotes pose little threat to humans. The problems generally start when people feed coyotes, even if that feeding is unintentional.*

The important word after the last bullet above is "most." Most coyotes do not attack humans, true, but some coyotes—or coywolves—attacked Taylor Mitchell in anticipation of eating her. The only other recorded human death by coyote was a three-year-old girl who died in August 1981 after a coyote hauled her off by the hand in an apparent act of predation. The youngster had walked out the door of her Glendale, California, home and was being dragged down the street when her father chased off the animal. The child died of a broken neck and blood loss. She was probably a target of opportunity, and in the coyote's eyes could have been any small prey animal.

Another such target was fortunate to survive. An animal described as a massive coywolf, weighing perhaps one hundred pounds, leapt upon a trampoline where a three-year-old girl was playing with her sister, in Randolph County, North Carolina, during 2011. The beast grabbed the girl's shirt and dragged her away. Seeing her daughter carried off "in the mouth of a monster," according to a local news report, the toddler's frantic mother jumped on the coywolf. Maternal fury won the day and the mother was able to free her daughter from the animal. Mother and children fled to the house and called for help. Before authorities arrived, a neighbor arrived with his shotgun and the coywolf, which refused to leave the yard, was dispatched.

Many biologists are coyote apologists, as are animal rightists, like those who claimed that the Glendale youngster who was dragged from her home by a coyote in 1981 was the victim of child abuse. Charges by the latter were in response to a coyote cull by the city. To put coyote attacks on people into perspective, according to the federal Centers for Disease Control and Prevention, almost five million people, about 2 percent of the population, are bitten by domestic dogs annually, at least ten, often more, fatally. An analysis of 142 coyote attacks on 159 victims in the United States and Canada from 1985 to 2006 by the Cook County Coyote Project, headed by Gehrt, found that an astonishing 37 percent were predatory. Seven percent were by rabid animals, 6 percent on people with pets, and only 4 percent resulted from the coyote feeling threatened. Twenty-two percent of the attacks involved coyotes biting a person at rest or sleeping. These incidents verge on predation, because they appear to be attempts to determine if the human was suitable prey. About half the attacks were in California, further evidence that the state has an immense number of people living close to wild terrain. An additional 24 percent of attacks went unclassified due to insufficient details. Odds are that at least some were predatory.

Granted, most victims were not seriously injured and were able to fight back or escape. The inescapable fact remains, however, that they were attacked. It is true that most coyotes do not attack people. Most people do not attack people, either. But serial killers, gangbangers, muggers, and other assorted savages do on a regular basis. So do some individual coyotes. The truth is that coyotes are far from the goofy cartoon character forever doomed to be outwitted by a roadrunner, but are instead highly efficient predators that live by killing a wide assortment of prey. If a person is vulnerable, it is natural for a coyote to look upon that individual as a potential meal. If the coyotes are of a bigger strain, numerous, or both, or if the object of their attention is small or incapacitated, the chances of a human falling prey increase markedly. Plainly and simply, if they think they can get away with it, many coyotes will try to prey on humans.

Attacks on people are increasing, and there are hints that urban coyotes, especially, are becoming more aggressive and dangerous. Evidence of this trend is an incident that occurred in the Chicago suburb of Riverside, Illinois, in 2013. Before dawn on a February morning, a homeowner let his three dogs into the backyard to do their business. Four coyotes suddenly charged from nearby bushes, jumped a fence, and went after the dogs. Their owner managed to get his dogs back into the house, but the coyote pack kept on coming. They leapt upon a door to the home, snarling and smashing glass panes until the homeowner shot at them with a high-powered air gun.

Two main reasons why coyotes are becoming more aggressive around people: plenty of food and not enough fear. Either because misguided people are deliberately feeding these animals, or accessible garbage has become easy pickings, coyotes are learning to associate humans with something to eat. "Coyotes may visit a home if they find food, water, or shelter there. Food can include unattended pets, birds or rodents attracted to bird feeders, pet food, garbage, or fallen fruit," advises the Arizona Game and Fish Department on its website. Constant exposure of coyotes to humans without being subject to hostile action, such as gunfire, eliminates fear. Most coyotes where I live scatter when they encounter people. A fair number of people where I leave hunt or trap coyotes. You will not find that kind of pressure on city streets or in suburbs where people do not—or cannot—hunt.

Attacks often come in flurries. "Concerns Grow over Coyotes," was the headline of a *Los Angeles Times* story on May 10, 2008, about coyote activity in the scenic resort community of Lake Arrowhead, outside Los Angeles. During late winter and early spring, coyotes grabbed two toddlers and entered a home where a third was playing. Adults drove off the animals. In a nearby community, a coyote yanked a toddler out of a sandbox, fleeing only when two adults intervened. Another headline, "3 Bitten in 24 Hours in Peoria Coyote Attacks," greeted the citizens of Phoenix after a trio of unprovoked attacks during March 2012 in Arizona's ninth-largest city by population. The coyotes involved seem to have a thing for people sitting on their porches, being that all three victims were so ensconced when attacked. During one week in June 2010, a pair of coyotes struck twice in the town of Rye, a Westchester County close-in suburb of New York City. In both cases, they bit young girls playing in their yards before being chased off. While a direct link cannot be proven, the attacks mentioned above coincide with the time of year that coyotes are denned up with pups. Like other animals, coyotes are especially protective when raising their young. They also hunt more actively because they have extra mouths to feed.

For as yet undefined reasons, some communities seem to be epicenters of coyote-on-human violence. While scanning the Internet for accounts of attacks, I found Boulder to be prominent. It seemed open season on joggers in Boulder, Colorado, for a time. Runners were bitten on trails during New Year's 2013 and a year before, in February. The earlier attack almost coincided with one on a father and child while they were out for a walk. In November 2011, authorities killed a coyote that had been snapping at bicyclists as they pedaled a Boulder bike path. Two coyotes were shot and killed in

March 2013 after they bit a five-year-old boy who was with a friend and his father in a public open-space area.

Especially when a coyote's instinct to defend its territory peaks while raising young, dogs become a primary target. Several people have become embroiled with coyotes while walking their dogs. To take a dog for a stroll in an area where coyotes are known to be aggressive is to take a risk akin to removing the Lone Ranger's mask or treading on Superman's cape. In New York, a Westchester County woman was bitten and scratched by a coyote in January 2010 while walking her dog in the town of Greenburgh. In March 2013, a female psychotherapist was walking her thirty-pound dog along a trail in—again—Boulder—when a coyote attacked it. The dog had to literally tear itself away from the coyote's teeth. The attacker fled when another person walking three larger dogs arrived. The area had been the scene of several coyote incidents, including the killing by officers of two coyotes involved in the March attack on the five-year-old boy described above. Coyotes in Boulder have become so bold with respect to dogs that one even jumped a pet in a dog park.

As one might suspect, smaller breeds such as diminutive terriers are often targets. When coyotes are riled up by protective instinct, however, dogs of any size may draw an assault. The Chicago researchers found that Labradors and golden retrievers were among the larger breeds commonly attacked. My bet is that these two breeds invite attack because many of them have been specifically bred for docility, to make them better pets, robbing them of the instinct to hunt that is their heritage. Labradors and goldens of this ilk are soft, the patsies of dogdom. As dogs, albeit wild ones, coyotes view their domestic kin as competitors, so they may do battle at any time of year. On a November day in 2011, a creature described as a large coyote attacked and killed a Great Dane in Newington, Connecticut. If you think that the name of the dog breed just mentioned was a misidentification, think again. It was a Great Dane, wounded so badly by a single coyote—or, rather, a coywolf—that a veterinarian could not save its life. The kill is a vivid measure of the strength and ferocity that coywolves can attain.

Unless seemingly ten feet high and topped by concertina wire, fences seem to do little against coyotes intent on sinking their fangs into dog meat. In 2011, a coyote grabbed fuzzy little white Muffin through a hole in a backyard fence and hauled her off, pink ribbon and all. With Muffin in its jaws, the coyote hopped another fence, of cinder block, before dropping the little dog's bloodied body in a neighbor's yard, where its distraught owner found it dead. Coyotes have jumped fences six feet high and more to get at dogs.

Coyotes enjoy dog food, both the kind that comes in bags and cans and the variety that comes on four legs and has a tail. Toy breeds are especially choice tidbits and, if coyotes are abroad, must be guarded with care when outside. An owner who lets out a dog like a Chihuahua on its own when coyotes are lurking, even if only in the backyard, might as well put it on a Ritz cracker.

The community impact of coyote depredations varies according to local experience. Again, cloistered neighborhoods of suburbs and cities where a rigorous outdoors experience is a walk in the park react differently from places where people are used to field dressing and butchering deer. Wellesley, Massachusetts, a posh immediate suburb of Boston, went into a furor, with residents expressing fear vocally, when coyotes attacked a few dogs during February 2012. When two pet dogs were attacked by coyotes in Chappaqua, New York, the elegant Westchester town where Bill and Hillary Clinton abide, townspeople were so upset they called a community meeting to deal with the crisis. When a dog disappears and is presumed to be killed by coyotes in my neck of the woods, it is a sad event, but most locals will add, "That's life."

There is one coyote that might rue the day it attacked a small dog in one ritzy Los Angeles neighborhood. It may have messed with the wrong pet owner. A cute little pup, Phoebe, disappeared in March 2013. Its owner offered a $10,000 reward for its safe return. In April, the dog's mangled body was found on the owner's property, apparently a coyote victim. The owner, like anyone who is attached to a beloved pet, was described as heartbroken by the press, which gave the incident extensive coverage. There was a reason. The owner was Sylvester Stallone.

Celebrity status is no protection against coyotes. During 2002 and 2003, residents of Greenwich, Connecticut, were swept by panic over marauding coyotes. Things got really scary when a coyote snatched a little bichon frise right off the backyard patio under the very eyes of Frank Gifford, who with his wife, Kathie Lee, owned the dog.

As far as cats are concerned, they are toast. In my neck of the woods, when a "missing cat" sign goes up at the little store that serves as the town post office, odds are the feline is not really lost but being digested by a coyote. Anyone who lets a pet cat roam in space shared by coyotes cares little for the welfare of the pet. Secretly, I suspect, some birders revel in the havoc wrought by coyotes on free-ranging felines because of the monstrous toll the cats take upon upland birds and songbirds, perhaps as many as one hundred million a year, according to some bird conservation groups. The situation puts animal protectionists in a quandary. They love cats and they love coyotes. How do you protect one without controlling the other? Often the answer is to contest the fact that coyotes eat cats, which is the ultimate in denial. Tell it to the East Naples, Florida, resident whose outdoor security camera filmed a coyote chasing her pet cat up a tree, knocking it to the ground, and chomping down on the poor feline.

Research described by Gehrt in November 2013 regarding feral—as opposed to pet—cats and coyotes may endear canids to animal protectionists and bird lovers. Feral cats tend to avoid urban green spaces such as parks and nature preserves when coyotes are roaming these areas. Instead, the cats concentrate around developed areas, such as housing and shopping centers. The result: much less predation by cats on wild birds.

Pet owners, parents, and urban residents in general need realize that coyotes are now a fact of their lives. Unlike cougars, which may become permanent residents on the fringes of urban areas but only visit downtown while occasionally passing through, coyotes readily adapt to the city. They find plenty of shelter in urban spaces and, most importantly, their omnivorous feeding habits are amply supported there.

Safety Tips: Coyotes

Virtually every state wildlife agency and many wildlife organizations offer suggestions for how to keep people and pets safe from coyotes. First of all, if coyotes are seen or heard in your vicinity, do not allow pets to be outside unsupervised, which is a bad idea under any circumstances. This is a commonsense measure, as is eliminating any source of food left outside. That means keeping a tight lid on trashcans containing edible garbage, and feeding pets indoors. Secure enclosures for poultry, rabbits, and other livestock. Low-lying branches, brush, and other ground-level debris can be utilized as hiding or den sites for coyotes—and their prey. Trimming and cleaning up tangled vegetation goes a long way toward keeping coyotes away. As noted, coyotes are experts at bypassing fences. Electric fencing can help, but it is more suited to pastureland for livestock than to backyards. Use it there and you risk zapping your neighbor's kids, which could lead to worse outcomes than any produced by coyotes.

Obviously, if there are coyotes in the immediate area, young children should never be allowed outside unsupervised. Children playing in groups provide no defense, because coyotes can target one child among several.

If coyotes regularly appear near your home, discourage them. Of course, the ultimate discouragement is a good, clean shot. If you opt for that method, you had better check local firearms and game laws. Loud noise works if a coyote has not grown overly confident around people. Instead of shouting, try banging together pots and pans. Or make a coyote shaker—a soda can filled with pebbles. Some wildlife experts advise spraying the animal with a hose. For my money, if a coyote comes close enough to allow you to spray it, you may be in more danger than a dousing with water can avert.

Once a coyote becomes aggressive, your options decrease. Here is what the Arizona Game and Fish Department, which obviously has considerable experience with coyotes, has to say about what to do next: "Don't turn away or run because the animal may view it as an opportunity to chase. Keep eye contact. Move towards other people, a building, or an area of activity." In other words, do not panic, but get out of the coyote's range.

If you are concerned about dangerous coyotes, your best recourse is to contact your local public safety authorities as well as your state wildlife agency. But do it only if you perceive a real threat. Do not call every time you catch sight of a coyote.

CHAPTER 5

THAT'S NOT BIG BIRD
AT YOUR FEEDER:
An Abundance of Bruins

H ad it been on a workday instead of Sunday, the closing
of the Massachusetts Turnpike by state police just west
of Boston at 7:27 A.M., even for just a few minutes, would
have had rush hour traffic snarled and drivers snarling. Even
so, motorists probably grumbled because there was no ap
parent cause for the blockage. No accident was in sight. Not
a construction worker anywhere. Just a short distance away,
however, a police officer was drawing a bead with a Reming-
ton Model 870 pump-action shotgun on a threat to public
safety that was about to be neutralized. Seconds later, on
June 2, 2013, a young American black bear was dead.

The bear, a small male weighing 125 pounds and probably little more than a yearling on his own for the first time,
was plugged by a state environmental police officer—trendy
name for a game warden—while it took refuge high in a tree
near the pike and above Massachusetts Bay Transportation
Authority (MBTA) commuter rail tracks. To get a clear shot
at the bear, the officer had to climb atop a ladder raised by a
Newton Fire Department truck. Although the environmental cops claimed that chances of tranquilizing instead of killing the bear were slim, given that it was masked by thick foliage, the agency took considerable heat from the Boston-area
public and news media for not trying an easier, softer method of solving the problem.

The fact that the excitement centered on the method used to eliminate the bear rather than on the bear itself, a real, live, wild bruin—and not one from the city's NHL franchise—only seven miles from downtown Boston, is a sign of the times. As in many other parts of the nation, bears are repopulating Massachusetts exponentially and wandering deep into metropolitan areas. Suburbanites and small-town dwellers throughout the country are growing accustomed to seeing creatures as large as Big Bird poking around for sunflower seeds intended for cardinals and finches.

By the middle of the nineteenth century, bears had been for all intents and purposes exterminated in the Bay State. Northern New England states such as Vermont retained a few bears, a reservoir that served as an eventual source of individuals to repopulate the southern portion of the region.

Beginning in the 1950s, bears began to filter into Massachusetts, mostly in rural areas west of the Connecticut River, from northern New England. The creatures prospered, increasing to about one hundred animals in the 1970s to almost forty times that number by the beginning of the twenty-first century. What is more, they emerged from the wilderness and became familiar sights even in the most populous parts of the state. Among them, Cape Cod, which may have lacked bears when the Pilgrims arrived, now has seen a bear or two prowling its pine barrens.

The first bear seen on the Cape since European settlement appeared in 2012, as Memorial Day visitors opened the summer season there. It was tranquilized, wrapped up in the heavy green netting that Massachusetts state conservation authorities use to trundle around captured bears, and relocated in the center of the state. A couple of weeks later, identified by a tag that had been placed in its ear, it showed up in Brookline, near Boston College, on the border of Boston proper, one hundred miles from its release site. Authorities carted away the bear again, this time to the westernmost reaches of the state.

The decline and eventual comeback of the bear in Massachusetts is typical of what has happened in most of the Lower 48 states, in which bears were exceedingly rare or even just a memory only a half century or so ago. Black bears once abounded from central Mexico to the Arctic tree line. As their ability to scramble high up in the boughs testifies, if trees are absent—as on plains, desert, and tundra—usually so are they. Like some of the other creatures discussed in this book, bears vanished as forests were cut and fragmented. Early settlers hunted them for food and pelts and as vermin. Davy Crockett was far from the only frontiersman who bragged about his bear-killing prowess.

In the Darwinian world of the frontier, bears existed to be killed. As the frontier faded, so did kill-or-be-killed attitudes. The development of a national conservation ethic caused bears to be elevated from vermin to a wildlife resource. They were protected when needed and, where they remained in sufficient numbers, managed as a game species subject to scientifically regulated hunting seasons. None of these factors alone account for the bear's resurgence. Combined, however, these developments prevented bears from sliding further toward oblivion and led to the long haul back to abundance. Their big break came as, in places like New England, farms were abandoned and the processes of natural succession promoted forest regrowth. An ironic twist to the harm that fossil fuels cause to the atmosphere is that their emergence reduced the need for wood as fuel, helping forests recover. Better forestry practices in general promoted regeneration of woodland, so many areas that had been logged returned to woodland. The dense forests that covered Vermont, for example, were 75 percent cleared by European settlers and loggers. Forest recovery there, however, began early, by the 1850s, allowing for bear recovery there.

The recovery of bears in northern New England had a domino effect. Since wildlife does not recognize political boundaries, Massachusetts bears wandered into Connecticut and seeded a population there. After more than a century of absence, bears began to return to Connecticut in the 1980s. One morning during that time frame, I found that during the night, my gas grill, parked next to the floor-to-ceiling windows on the south side of my home, had been destroyed. The angle irons holding up the food tray on the grill had been bent like pretzels; I could not straighten out the bend even though I tried with all my strength. The wooden slats of the tray had been detached and were covered with deep groves, obviously caused by claws; the scratches had a span larger than my hand. Just by chance, a game warden friend happened by later that day. I showed him the grill and joked about a "big raccoon." He replied with a wink: "Some raccoon." Bear numbers are growing so quickly that Connecticut state wildlife authorities will only estimate that there are "hundreds," at least five hundred, in the state. More than three thousand bear damage reports and sightings are reported annually.

The story of bear recovery is similar throughout the rest of the United States and has continued apace. At least forty-three states have resident—which means reproducing as well as living in area—populations of black bears. The creatures are common in about twenty-nine of these states and show signs of increasing in others. Most range maps show them missing from prairie states and central midwestern states like Kansas and Indiana, but not for long, because reports of sightings are starting to be made in these areas. Bears were almost exterminated, if not completely removed, from Texas by the 1940s. Bears have been edging into East

Texas from neighboring states since about the 1970s. They also have been moving into West Texas from New Mexico and adjacent mountains south of the Mexican border. One of those states, Arkansas, was once known as the Bear State, but lost almost all its bears. The recovery of bears there received help from the state wildlife agency, which began to reintroduce the species with transplants from the northern Midwest and Canada during 1959. By the 1980s it had enough bears to begin a hunting season. Arkansas bears have also edged into Missouri, starting to renew the lost population there. Alabama and Mississippi have a handful of bears that have spilled over from adjacent states, and their populations promise to grow.

Bear encounters have become so frequent that on August 8, 2012, *USA Today* ran a story called "Summer of the Bear" that was a roundup of bear-human encounters that season.

From the standpoint of people who enjoy nature, bears are a welcome addition to local fauna. But it comes at a price. Where there are lots of bears and lots of people, the interests of bruin and human often conflict. Forget about Yogi, Smokey, the Three Bears, and cute bears that promote toilet tissue in television advertisements. Make no mistake about it. A black bear bent on killing humans is a terrifying beast. No better example exists of the naked savagery of a black bear attack than an incident in April 2006, near a campground in the Cherokee National Forest of Tennessee. A four-hundred-pound black bear emerged from the woods and charged a family that had been playing near a waterfall. The bear grabbed the young son in its jaws, critically wounding him, as it did the boy's mother when she tried to fight it off. Onlookers came running and pelted the bear with rocks and sticks until it ran off. Meanwhile, the family's six-year-old girl panicked and fled. The bear apparently caught up with her; a county fire and rescue officer found the bear standing over her corpse. When the bear charged him, the officer fired at it with a handgun and it ran off.

Equally scary was the attack of a black bear on a fifty-four-year-old woman in Longwood, Florida, as she walked her two dogs on December 2, 2013. Newspaper accounts described a snarling bear that repeatedly knocked down the woman and savagely bit her head and face. She was finally able to break free and run to a neighbor's house. Reuters, in a news dispatch, described the incident as "the worst reported bear attack on a human in Florida history" (Decembers 31, 2013)

Officials later said the bear might have been trying to protect its three cubs. A two-hundred-pound bear believed to be the attacker was later trapped and destroyed by wildlife officials.

Weighing up to six hundred pounds but averaging less than half that size, black bears are powerful, potentially dangerous animals that have attacked and killed a goodly number of humans, sometimes in order to eat them. Treating a black bear like a weak sister of the bigger, fiercer grizzly tempts fate. The image fostered by naive nature-programming on television, of black bears as the furry clowns of the animal world, is a myth, and a perilous one to believe. Black bears have killed dozens of people since 1900, at least as many as brown bears, including the grizzly. Attacks by black bears on humans exceed those by brown bears, but that is a function of the abundance of the former and their proximity to large numbers of humans.

My 1976 book *Killer Animals: The Menace of Animals in the World of Man* (back then, editors still allowed the noun denoting the male gender to stand for everybody) examined the qualities and circumstances that make animals dangerous to people. In the section on bears, I wrote about a rampage by black bears in Alaska during the summer of 1963. Totally unprovoked, the bears attacked four people, killing one. I cited the wisdom of the time that the reason for the attacks was unclear, although the bears might have been driven by hunger due to a poor crop of wild blueberries, a staple for them at that time of year. The implication was that if tho attacks were actually attempts to get a meal, the episode was a fluke. Both animal rightists and bear researchers who become emotionally attached to their subjects tend to paint black bears in a nonpredatory light as far as attacks on humans are concerned. They sometimes argue that consumption of human flesh by bears is simply opportunistic, as in the case of a bear that ate the corpse of a paroled murderer during 2012 in British Columbia. The man had apparently died while drinking and drugging in his vehicle, which was parked on a logging road. The bear found the body and dragged it from the vehicle into the brush. After authorities discovered the ravaged corpse, they killed the bear, fearing it might have acquired a taste for human flesh.

Since 2011, apologists for black bear predation on people have had a problem. A study released that year by a respected guru of bear behavior trashed the idea that attacks on humans by hungry bears are an aberration. Dr. Stephen Herrero of the University of Calgary found that 88 percent of the sixty-three people he recorded as killed by black bears in North America between 1900 and 2009 were killed for food. (While this chapter was being written, in June 2013, the number of people killed by black bears went up one, to sixty-four. The victim was a man in his sixties killed outside his cabin in George Lake, Alaska. The cabin was in remote wilderness, but the attack conceivably could have happened in any suburban backyard where bears search for birdseed or garbage.) The study, published in the prestigious *Journal of Wildlife Management,* also cast doubt on another hallowed idea about aggressive bears. Ninety-two percent of the predatory attacks were by males, not mothers defending their cubs, as traditional wisdom has held. "The common belief that surprising a mother bear with cubs is the most dangerous kind of black bear encounter is inaccurate," Herrero maintained, as quoted in a University of Calgary press release in May 2011. Claiming that the results surprised even him, Herrero explained, "Most fatal bear attacks were predatory and all fatal attacks were carried out by a single bear."

Not surprisingly, most of the fatal attacks have happened since the 1960s, when bears were beginning to recover, and more than 20 percent since 2000. More deaths occurred in Canada and Alaska than in the Lower 48.

Herrero did not explain why most fatalities occurred outside the Lower 48, which is odd considering that more bears and fewer people live in Alaska and Canada than to the south, so there is less contact between *Ursus americanus* and *Homo sapiens*. He suggested one possibility: northern habitat is less productive and may experience periodic food shortages, which, according to a quote attributed to Herrero in the University of Calgary press release, "may predispose some bears to consider people as prey."

At the same time, the study indicated that rising bear attacks go hand in hand with "human population growth." As with the greater incidence of attacks in the North, Herrero said, again as quoted in the press release, "We didn't demonstrate why population growth is correlated with more bear attacks but we suspect it is because there are more people pursuing recreational and commercial activities in black bear habitat." I suspect this is correct, and that many of these people are new to the woods and have a perception of wild animals shaped by Disney and *Born Free*.

My own take on all of this is that there have been more attacks in Canada and Alaska in total because until recently not enough bears lived in the Lower 48 to make an impact. If, as Herrero says, attacks rise with human numbers, then expect the scales to tip toward attacks in the cities and suburbs that are being infiltrated by bears.

Like most other researchers who deal with bear attacks, Herrero noted that while black bears do pose a risk, it is low. "Each year there are millions of interactions between people and black bears with no injuries to people," he is quoted in the University of Calgary press release announcing the study. The problem is, however, that the chances of being that one-in-a-million victim are bound to mount as black bears increasingly prowl backyards and parks. So are the chances of encounters between bears and humans, simply because there are more humans as well as bears. Since black bears began their comeback, 145 million people have been added to the United States and Canada, a fact that was pointed out by U.S. Fish and Wildlife Service bear expert Chris Servheen at an international workshop on human-bear conflicts in Missoula, Montana, in 2012.

It seems counter to conventional conservation wisdom that a big carnivore should experience a population boom while people are doing the same. But this is what is happening. Between 1988 and 2011, according to Servheen, black bears increased by 17.6 percent. The number of North American black bears surpasses that of all the other six bear species worldwide combined. Estimates of black bear numbers in North America creep upward every year. High-end estimates close in on a million animals, with a little more than half in Canada and the rest in the United States. Perhaps two hundred thousand of the United States' bears inhabit Alaska. Conservative estimates hover at about seven hundred thousand animals, so either way you look at it, there are lots of bears.

Ironically, perhaps, it may be the converse of wilderness preservation that is helping bears prosper; that is, urbanization. The reasons can be found tucked away in a major study by Hank Hristienko of Manitoba Conservation, the provincial environmental agency, and John E. McDonald Jr. of the U.S. Fish and Wildlife Service, that was published in the journal *Ursus* in 2007. Among the factors the authors credit with making the world a better place for black bears is a bane of modern sportsmen, myself included. It is that the amount of private land to which hunters have access is shrinking by the day. Speaking from my own experience, acres and acres of land I once roved with shotgun in hand are now occupied by housing developments and, in some cases, horse farms, whose owners, perhaps understandably, have posted their property. Another reason, linked to a reduction of hunting, is that more and more municipalities have enacted restrictions on the discharge of firearms within their jurisdiction.

On the other hand, the erection of suburbs on land that was once forest and field does not necessarily reduce the capability of habitat to support bears, the authors suggest. Black bears are like coyotes in the way in which they readily adapt to a wide variety of changes in their environment. City bears may be bigger and fatter than country bears because of the amenities provided by urban living. It just may be tougher for bears to earn a living off the land beyond the burbs. According to Hristienko and McDonald, "Suburban woodland areas are becoming sanctuaries for bears, primarily because they provide food in the absence of risks (to bears)." No question that city bears find food within easy walking distance. Like coyotes, bears in urban areas need less home territory to find food. Bears with exposure to human concentrations in Nevada, according to a study by Jon Beckmann and Carl Lackey in the Fall 2008 issue of *Human–Wildlife Conflicts,* needed 10 percent to 30 percent of the home ranges required by wildland bears. Besides that, their body mass was 30 percent higher, they had more success reproducing, and needed less time denned up in winter. There is another plus that urban living has for bears: plenty of supplemental food, in the form of home vegetable gardens and fruit trees, compost piles, garbage, and birdseed. Unlike wild foods, those provided in backyards are year-round, rather than seasonal, sources of energy.

Hoping to find out why bears go to town, Colorado State University researchers tracked bears around Aspen, Colorado, where humans have swarmed into bear country, for five years ending in 2010. Trash was not a bear necessity in the area, the researchers found, suggesting that the animals prefer wild berries and acorns. "When natural resources were lean," said CSU scientist Ken Wilson, quoted in a July 20, 2010, research-news story on the CSU website, "bears were creative and resourceful enough to track down more easily attainable human food." Their findings are consistent with episodes in other parts of the country during which bears more commonly sought food in towns when drought depleted wild nuts and berries. Insufficient natural food sources in the Great Smoky Mountains National Park in the fall of 2006 made bears more aggressive panhandling food from visitors. Dry late-summer weather in the same year sent bears into the city of Thunder Bay, Ontario, scavenging for food.

The Colorado researchers suggested that bears do not become garbage addicts, but return to natural food sources when these are available. This finding may seem counter to research indicating that once bears find easy pickings due to human activity, they rely on these sources. The prize for the most enterprising Colorado raider may go to a bear that, in August 2012, found its way through a partly opened deadbolt and cleaned out a candy story in Estes Park. According to newspaper reports, the bear made seven trips in and out of the store in about a quarter hour.

In raiding human space for food, bears have increased their already solid numbers in the areas around Reno and

Carson City, Nevada, and the Lake Tahoe Basin on the Nevada-California border. A 2013 study from the Wildlife Conservation Society (WCS) and the Nevada Department of Wildlife, under lead author Carl Lackey, revealed that a growing number of bear-human conflicts in the region stemmed both from people moving into bear country and bears entering settled areas, the two-way traffic described earlier in this book.

The more people come into the area, the more food is available for bears; the more food, the more bears. Reports of hungry bears in the Tahoe area doing damage and ransacking dwellings, many of them vacation homes, number in the thousands since the beginning of this century. News reports tell of bears learning to twist open doorknobs and mother bears teaching young to raid garbage containers. To complicate matters, heated debate has erupted between wildlife managers using hunting seasons to control bears, and residents, many who are not native Nevadans, who are horrified over bear killings.

WCS scientists also found that suburban bears who grow fat on a diet of what amounts to junk food "live fast and die young," to quote a description of the Tahoe-area study released by the organization. Urbanized bears that ate garbage weighed 30 percent more than wildland counterparts. They also were reproductively precocious, giving birth up to five years earlier than the seven- to eight-year-old average in the wild. As often happens in the city, they also died much younger, often violently, mostly in traffic accidents.

Through the course of the year, bear activity has peaks and valleys. In most of their range, they are least active in winter, when they spend considerable time sleeping in their dens. Their winter sleep is often described as hibernation but it is not, at least from a purely technical standpoint. Although the bear's breathing, heartbeat, and metabolism slows down, body temperature remains just about ten degrees below normal. The body temperature of true hibernators such as marmots drops almost to freezing and breathing and heartbeat are barely discernible. Bears can wake up at any time and, when spring comes, they are wide-eyed almost immediately.

Spring is a bustling time for bears as they replenish body fat off which they have lived during winter's lean times. Bears typically lose 25 percent of their body weight over the winter. The figure rises to 40 percent for reproductive females; adult females typically produce two or three cubs every two years, in January or February. Normally, bears awaken just in time for the appearance of natural foods such as certain berries. Climate change, however, could throw that harmonious arrangement out of whack. Weather, not the availability of food, is the bear's alarm clock. After the warm winter of 2012, New Hampshire wildlife authorities asked homeowners to take down birdfeeders two weeks early, on March 15 instead of April 1.

Even after they fill up, bears continue to actively move about. From late June into July, adult males are casting about for mates. Meanwhile, about the same time, young bears, in their second summer, are leaving their mothers. Males, usually under pressure from adult males, wander far and wide. Young females often settle down near the territories of their mothers but sometimes experience wanderlust. A young female captured after traipsing through the backyards of Greenwich, Connecticut, had a tag in its ear identifying it as a Jersey bear. To reach Greenwich, it had to have crossed the Hudson River and traveled through the heart of metropolitan New York City suburbia. One wonders if it took the George Washington or Tappan Zee Bridge.

The return of the black bear in New Jersey typifies the trend. Say "New Jersey" and you think of the Jersey Turnpike clogged with traffic, honky-tonk boardwalks on the beach, a maze of highways and tunnels funneling into Manhattan, and the suburban homes of New York City gangsters, real as well as fictional. True enough, perhaps, but New Jersey has the vast Pine Barrens in the south, and in the northwest corner, where the Delaware River enters from New York and separates Jersey from Pennsylvania, lie wild mountains and valleys as beautiful as any in the Northeast, or elsewhere, for that matter. There, especially in parklands, preserves, and refuges, black bears persisted long after vanishing from the rest of the state.

Until 1953, even those remaining black bears were considered vermin, subject to a year-round open season. Then it became a game animal, and hunting was sharply curtailed before being closed in 1971. Bears from the Northwest, as well as Pennsylvania and New York State, expanded southward and eastward. To control bear numbers, hunting season has been reopened, although not without cries of protest from the animal rights community. Bears have been seen in all twenty-one New Jersey counties, even in the Bergen County community of Fort Lee, the western entrance to the George Washington Bridge. Only the Hudson River separates Manhattan from Jersey's bears. Near Fort Lee, bears have visited Paramus, cluttered by one of the world's highest concentrations of shopping malls. A few bears have even been seen in Cape May, southernmost point in the state, which would be below the Mason-Dixon Line if that boundary did not jog south after leaving Pennsylvania. Bears have wandered onto the campus of Princeton University. In the commuter town of Randolph, during May 1913, residents of one neighborhood locked themselves in their homes at the urging of local authorities after a mother and cubs were observed strolling the streets.

New Jersey has so many bears that state wildlife authorities receive thousands of complaints and reports of bear sightings annually. In 2012, there were 734 sightings and 1,460 nuisance and damage reports.

Some encounters between bears and people contain a touch of humor, some of it necessarily black, no pun intended. In Hopatcong, forty miles west of Manhattan, a cable television repairman found a five-hundred-pound bear sound asleep in the basement of a customer's house. Neither the owners, the cable guy, or wildlife officials could determine how the bear had entered the house he'd chosen for his snooze. A young bear in Bakersfield, California, sent elementary school students scurrying for cover when it interrupted a May 2012 outdoor graduation. No one was hurt. The bear was tranquilized and relocated. The victim may not have found it funny, but obviously a *Miami Herald* editor did when he headlined a March 21, 2012, story "Wild Bear Bites Dog Owner in Butt." It happened in the central Florida city of Longwood. The owner, a woman, had her dog on a leash while putting some of the pet's poop in an outdoor garbage container. When a bear and cub approached, the woman fell backwards, with the bear staring down at her. She rolled over to escape and received a bite on the rump. She afterwards expressed thanks that it was only her backside that suffered.

The smattering of comedy involved in bear attacks is overshadowed by tragedy. Bear attacks are terrifying, especially since they usually take the victims by surprise. A thirty-year-old man who had just moved from Toronto to the town of Cochrane in central Ontario had the shock of his life—almost ending his life—while breakfasting on the porch of his new cabin. Out of nowhere a black bear rushed him. The man sought refuge in the cabin until the bear, after killing the man's German shepherd dog, decided to enter through the window. The victim then ran from the cabin, but the bear—black bears can run more than thirty miles an hour—ran him down and sank fangs into his skull. The

THAT'S NOT BIG BIRD AT YOUR FEEDER

man would have been a goner had not two women, driving by, scared off the bear by honking their car horn. The victim survived and was hospitalized.

The Alaskan man killed outside his cabin in 2013, referred to earlier in this chapter, was not so lucky. He was killed and partly eaten while his terrified wife hid traumatized in the cabin. After state troopers arrived, they saw a bear stalking them as they observed the body. They killed the bear, which had remains of the victim in its stomach.

Home and hearth are no guarantee of refuge from a bear on the prowl. In October 2011, a bear of a man and his wife fought off a bear that committed a vicious home invasion of their Newport, Pennsylvania, premises. The bear, perhaps protecting cubs, entered on the tail of the family dog when Rich Moyer, six feet, six inches tall and three hundred pounds, opened the door to let in the pet. Bear and man battled on the floor while Moyer's wife tried to help her husband. The bear jumped her, while Moyer wrestled with it, only to have the animal bite down on his skull, a wound later requiring seventy stiches to close. Moyer, using his large size to advantage, was able to battle the bear until it retreated from the house.

Courage rather than size enabled a seventy-two-year-old Vail, Colorado, woman to scare off a bear after she found it in her kitchen looking for pot roast. The bear smacked her on the chest and arm, gouging flesh with its claws. Undeterred, the woman clapped her hands and shouted, scaring the animal out the door. The drama did not end there. The woman soon found a cub still inside the home, which she booted out as well.

In September 2012, authorities killed a bear in Madison, Connecticut, the town next to mine, after it had repeatedly chased people into their homes. People described it as totally unafraid of humans. Connecticut bears seem to be predisposed to home invasions. One afternoon in June 2002, a resident of an apartment complex in the community of Winsted noticed the back end of a bear sticking out of his kitchen. The bear had apparently pushed aside an unlocked sliding screen door. Once inside, the shaggy intruder grabbed the kitchen garbage can and pulled it outside, onto a patio. It ate the contents, then ambled away into nearby woods.

Retreating into the house probably did save a woman in West Hartford, Connecticut, not far from Winsted, from suffering more than bites and scratches on her lower leg when attacked by a bear in May 2013. A female bear, accompanied by two cubs, went after the woman's small terrier just outside her home. She was attacked while trying to protect her pet. After reaching the safety of her house, she called 911. The bear, which had climbed a tree, was euthanized; the cubs were relocated in woodland. A seventy-two-year-old woman in the tiny city of McGregor, Minnesota, did not make it to the house when a bear jumped her in her backyard as she was taking her dog out early on an evening in June 2013. As she opened the door, the three yearling bears ran from under the back porch. The dog gave chase and the mother bear, just out of view, came to their rescue. As the woman tried to bring her dog back, the mother bear turned on her, knocking her to the ground and biting her arm. Fortunately for the woman, the bear ceased its attack and ran off after the cubs. The bears had apparently been after seed in a birdfeeder.

As these attacks demonstrate, black bears have no qualms about attacking and even killing people on their own doorsteps. The fatal attack described above admittedly occurred at a cabin deep in the Alaskan wilderness. Any of the attacks in the towns and cities just discussed could very well have turned deadly had not good fortune intervened. No longer is the potential for fatal attack by black bears a wilderness phenomenon. It now can happen next door, or even at your door.

Safety Tips: Bears

Authorities at national parks, national forests, and similar places where people recreate in the wild have long provided advice on how to stay safe when bears are about. Now, those suggestions merit attention from people living far from wilderness but who may be in proximity to black bears. Whether in a gated community or a far wilderness campsite, the number one rule is to keep the place clean. Food, garbage, and aromatic items like toothpaste and other toiletries in the trash will attract bears. Obviously, keep containers of garbage and trash secure. A rinsing every week or so with ammonia will minimize residual odors in trashcans. And it goes without saying, do not feed bears: they may literally bite the hand that does so. Keep barbecue grills clean if left outdoors. Better yet, bring them inside. If you have garbage pickup, do not put items out the night before. Do it in the morning. As with coyotes and cougars, thick brush near a home may offer a bear concealment, so if you want to be super safe, cut it. One bit of advice that is difficult for birders to take is to remove birdfeeders from the yard at winter's end. I do not do so, nor do I do much brush cutting around my home. My place is surrounded by woodland and swamp; that's why I moved there.

I have surveyed page after page of bear safety literature for homeowners from wildlife and parks agencies. The best advice I have found is from the website of the the New Jersey Division of Fish & Wildlife, adapted here:

- *Never* feed or approach a bear.
- Remain calm if you encounter a bear.
- Make the bear aware of your presence by speaking in an assertive voice, singing, clapping your hands, or making other noises.

- Make sure the bear has an escape route. If a bear enters your home, provide it with an escape route by propping all doors open.
- Avoid direct eye contact, which may be perceived by a bear as a challenge. Never run from a bear. Instead, slowly back away.
- To scare the bear away, make loud noises by yelling, banging pots and pans, or using an air horn. Make yourself look as big as possible by waving your arms. If you are with someone else, stand close together with your arms raised above your heads.
- The bear may utter a series of huffs, make popping jaw sounds by snapping its jaws, and swat the ground. These are warning signs that you are too close. Slowly back away, avoid direct eye contact, and do not run.
- If a bear stands on its hind legs or moves closer, it may be trying to get a better view or detect scents in the air. It is usually not a threatening behavior.
- Black bears will sometimes "bluff charge" when cornered, threatened, or attempting to steal food. Stand your ground, avoid direct eye contact, then slowly back away; again, do not run.
- If the bear does not leave, move to a secure area.
- Families who live in areas frequented by black bears should have a "Bear Plan" in place for children, with an escape route and planned use of whistles and air horns.
- Black bear attacks are extremely rare. If a black bear does attack, fight back!

CHAPTER 6

DEADLIEST OF ALL?
Dangerous Deer
and Marauding Moose

The creature that best qualifies as the most dangerous animal in North America is not any of the continent's venomous serpents, although these include some snakes whose venom ranks them among the world's most toxic. It is not the grizzly bear, black bear, or cougar, or, for that matter, the alligator, although all of these species kill and injure humans on a regular, if infrequent, basis. It does not have claws that rip and rend or a jaw equipped with canine fangs for piercing and tearing flesh. In fact, it never eats flesh, much less people, and does not even have upper canine teeth, or any other dentition remotely like fangs. Front incisor teeth are also missing from the upper jaw of its long, narrow muzzle. Instead, a pliant cartilaginous pad in the fore of its palate helps grasp shoots and leaves torn off and collected by its lower incisors, then swallowed and later regurgitated and chewed as cud. The vegan diet, soulful brown eyes, and graceful mien of the most dangerous animal in North American belies the toll it enacts on humans: thousands of injuries and about two hundred deaths annually. Beyond that, it enables the spread of a horrendous disease that afflicts thousands of people nationwide at any one time.

The most dangerous animal in North America is, if you have not already guessed, real-life Bambis. As they undertake their daily routine, nibbling vegetation as they go, deer cause all sorts of collateral damage. They leave in their wake mangled heaps of metal that were once cars and trucks and, often, mangled drivers and passengers as well; victims stricken with the fever and often-excruciating pain of Lyme disease; and woodlands stripped of their understory and biodiversity due to deers' overly eager browsing, which also makes short work of plants in gardens and landscaping.

There is nothing novel about deer eating crops. They have been eating up gardens since people first learned to till the soil. Their status as a major threat to human life and limb, on the other hand, is something attained only in a matter of decades, at least in scope. It reflects the volcanic explosion in population that deer have undergone during the last five or six decades, especially places where human numbers also have soared.

Deer also have an impact on other wildlife, which in turn can create problems for people. As noted in an earlier chapter, more deer means more cougars, which can subsist on small creatures but prosper best when they have access to bulk meat on the hoof. Thus, the abundance of deer is in part the reason that cougars are overflowing their western strongholds. The ten million human hunters who pursue buck and doe each year also have taken advantage of the bounty of burgeoning herds of deer, annually taking approximately six million of them. Despite all that pressure, neither humans nor cougars nor coywolves nor wolves have managed to put a dent in the nation's immense deer population. By conservative estimate, the number of deer in the United States today—thirty million—is five or six times the number in the early 1900s and approaches the population size when Europeans first arrived on the continent.

Writers who ponder the nation's deer numbers and ramifications thereof often ignore taxonomy. They discuss "deer" as if there were but one species in the Lower 48 when, except for about one hundred woodland caribou in the Selkirk Mountains of Washington, in reality there are two: the whitetail and the mule deer. The mule deer *(Odocoileus hemionus)* is a western species, found in arid and mountainous areas that the white-tailed deer *(Odocoileus virginianus)* generally avoids. Whitetails are virtually absent from California, Nevada, and Utah, but perhaps not for long, because elsewhere they are outcompeting and hybridizing with mule deer, which are less adaptable, and much younger from an evolutionary standpoint. Numbering about four million, mule deer are far fewer than their close cousins the whitetail, and may be declining.

White-tailed deer have been hunted since humans arrived in North America during the latter stages of the Pleistocene, the time of the ice ages. Fossils suggest that whitetails were here two million or three million years before that. Mule deer, which probably evolved from a western population of whitetails in a pocket of dry badlands and mountains, may not have even predated humans on the continent. Some researchers suggest they achieved their present form only twelve thousand years ago, but the general census is that they are older, although still extant for less than a million years. By hybridizing with whitetails, they may be evolving in reverse. Whenever the two species evolved, their relationship with people is so similar that what can be said for the whitetail covers the mule deer as well.

Almost as soon as Europeans began to settle what is now the United States, hunting pressure upon whitetails began to diminish their population. Meat to eat and hides for clothing—and before long hides for commerce as well as personal use—were the motivation. One theory about the origin of the term *buck* as used for the dollar is that in early days of settlement a deer hide was worth a Spanish dollar, the silver coin also called a piece of eight. James Fenimore

Cooper did not pick the name Deerslayer for his hero Natty Bumppo out of thin air, but because the nickname fit. If you were a frontiersman, you were a deer hunter, and Bumpo was the best of them all, so gained his title. When deer became scarce among the settlements, frontier hunters, one of my wife's ancestors among them, went over the Appalachians on "long hunts" spanning months, during which they cleaned up on—and cleaned out—deer from the forests. Traders paid Native Americans, who had subsistence-hunted deer since the ice ages, to kill as many as possible, taking a toll of about five million deer a year. Within a century of European settlement, deer in places like North Carolina flirted with extinction.

All the while, agriculture and logging, especially in North Woods terrain too rocky for farming, replaced forest and deer habitat. Eventually, states such as Connecticut were border-to-border farmland, with little cover and forage to support deer. The whitetail was so rare there that a sighting made the newspapers. In 1842, only one deer was killed in the state, in the city of Waterbury, where I was raised. By the turn of the century, only a couple of dozen inhabited the entire state. About three hundred deer inhabited a refuge about fifteen miles wide on Cape Cod in Massachusetts, with the only other deer there a handful in the Berkshire Mountains abutting New York and Vermont. So few deer remained in Vermont that the hunting season was closed by 1865. Neither Pennsylvania nor New Jersey had more than a few stragglers. New York's only deer hid in the heart of the great North Woods of the central Adirondacks. As settlers, hunters, loggers, and agriculture marched west, deer numbers dwindled through the rest of the country as well. By the early twentieth century, there were only five hundred deer in Arkansas, a state famed for its wild and woolly country and wildlife abundance.

Deer recovered and then thrived for many of the same reasons as have other creatures now adapting to life among humans: return of second-growth forest to cleared land; reduction of predators; conservation laws and ethic; favorable manipulation of habitat by wildlife managers; and restocking of lost populations. Deer not only benefited from the evolution of conservation ethic but helped inspire establishment of wildlife laws and management. Just as they are today, deer were a magnet for hunters, who basically consisted of two groups. As in Great Britain, where people of means and blue blood traditionally engage in "stalking deer," one group consisted of wealthy sportsmen, city based, who took breaks from building railroads and mills to engage in wilderness hunts. The Adirondacks of northern New York, for example, were where the Vanderbilts, Carnegies, and other industrial barons went hunting and camping. Their "camps" were staffed by chefs from Manhattan and liveried servants. Their hunting excursions were the basis of an entire industry, the Adirondack guides. In Pennsylvania, the Poconos attracted the well-heeled from Philadelphia and Pittsburgh. The other group of deer hunters was basically the good ole boys, locals who hunted largely for survival rather than sport, although enjoyment may have been a side benefit.

During the second half of the nineteenth century, these two disparate socioeconomic groups were suddenly confronted by the same unpleasant reality. The deer were about gone, but the stage was set for a comeback. Deer predators had vanished, too. Better yet, the tide of habitat destruction had turned in the hinterlands. Second-growth woodland, with abundant understory browse for deer, was reclaiming farmland. It also was covering terrain where loggers had leveled mature forests, which even when healthy do not support as many deer as emergent woodland.

A powerful constituency arose that sought restoration of

deer herds. With deer as a potent, although not sole, motivating force, state and federal laws and management programs to conserve wildlife began to appear during the last quarter of the nineteenth century. State game agencies, the ancestors of environmental protection and environmental conservation departments, were formed to oversee hunting and fishing: the Pennsylvania Game Commission in 1895, the appointment of three state agents called "game protectors" by New York in 1880. At the same time, as for no other animal, wealthy hunters reached into their pockets to purchase vast tracts of deer country in places such as the Adirondacks to keep it intact, for them at least. Locals were barred, although many followed the example of Robin Hood, creating more than a few confrontations between rich and poor. Eventually most such private lands became public, bolstering state and federal holdings that were growing like Topsy.

Meanwhile, the new state game agencies and, again, sportsmen began to transplant deer from the few surviving populations. During the early 1900s, Pennsylvania purchased and released more than a thousand deer from other states. Deer restoration marched south and west from the Northeast, where it had mostly begun, and in 1937 received a positive jolt of energy from federal funding. That year, Congress passed the Pittman-Robertson Federal Aid in Wildlife Restoration Act, which channeled an excise tax on sporting arms and ammunition to the states. Much of that money went to deer restoration, justified partly by the fact that healthy deer habitat means good habitat for a variety of other species as well.

It is a pun, admittedly, but I submit that no other native North American species has been the beneficiary of more big-conservation bucks over the long term than the white-tailed deer. The cash flow continues today. Small wonder. Deer hunting is the basis of a huge industry. There are a zillion organizations—such as Whitetails Unlimited—that support deer hunting and conservation. Deer hunting is the focus of more specialty hunting publications than any other game species. Deer hunters spend money not only at sporting goods stores and gun shops but at motels, gas stations, photography shops, truck and off-road vehicle dealers, and online suppliers of outdoor equipment. Just how much deer hunters spend may come as a surprise even to hunters. The National Shooting Sports Foundation, a firearms-industry trade organization based in Newtown, Connecticut, estimates that in just one year surveyed, 2006, deer hunters coughed up $12.4 billion on their sport. That is four times the amount spent on hunting small game such as rabbits and upland birds. I am a hunter, but have never been gripped by the mystique of the deer hunt the way it enthralls some of my good friends. Some of them approach it with the fervor of religionists.

As do religions, deer-hunting believers include zealots for whom there is no greater dogma than insuring the abundance, even overabundance, of their quarry. They brook no competition from four-footed competitors, demanding elimination of predators without heed to the ecological imbalance that results. Supplemental feeding, especially in winter, is a basic tenet of their faith and carried on by some public agencies as well as sportsmen. Providing deer with what is in effect a soup kitchen can be counterproductive. "What seems like a good idea can often do more harm than good," the Utah Division of Wildlife Resources says of the practice on its website. Feeding stations, according to a position statement issued by the Maine Department of Inland Fisheries and Wildlife, "may disrupt deer migration to natural wintering areas" and concentrate deer where predators can home in on them. Worse yet, if deer are fed within a half mile of roads, collisions with motor vehicles increase "significantly."

The last thing needed on the nation's highways is a practice that leads to more vehicular smashups with deer. A study by the insurance company State Farm estimated that an accident between a deer and a motor vehicle occurs every twenty-six seconds. Another State Farm study estimated that there were 1.23 million deer–motor vehicle accidents during the year ending June 30, 2012. Damage from these accidents was about $4 billion. As for injuries, the annual count is about thirty thousand. Just for comparison, in 2012, sharks attacked fifty-three people in the United States, including Puerto Rico and Hawaii, according to the International Shark Attack File at the Florida Museum of Natural History.

Figures may reveal the scope of the problem but not the individual tragedies and heartache. Deer can enter a roadway so quickly that even a trained race driver operating in daylight may not be able to avoid a crash. This happened in August 2006 at a track in Wisconsin when a Brazilian driver was putting his open-wheel racer through a test run. Cristiano da Matta was hospitalized for a ruptured blood vessel on the brain after his car smacked into a deer that bolted out of woods alongside the track. Given that accident, the odds are against the average driver in a similar situation. Deer can emerge onto the roadside almost as if they had been teleported there.

Once a deer makes the transition between the highway margin and the roadway, their behavior is difficult to predict. More often than not, however, the deer will bound across the road and disappear into woods or fields on the opposite side. Deer-wary drivers know enough to keep their foot on the brake and eyes on the roadside even after a deer clears the roadway. Odds are good that one or more of a thundering herd is following in the first one's hoofprints. Occasionally, an encounter can literally cause a case of deer in the headlights. The deer may be confused or curious and simply freeze.

Many years ago, on the woods-lined road in front of my home, I had such an encounter at two o'clock in the morning while I was in the backseat of a taxicab. After several weeks on assignment in Africa, I had landed at JFK in New York City, then taken an airport limo to a terminal in New Haven. I called a cab from the terminal to take me the thirty additional miles to my home. There are few houses on the road near where I live, which is bounded mostly by woods. Just before the turn into my driveway, a buck—I still remember it had an impressive set of antlers—appeared out of the darkness and stopped in the middle of the road. Unused to dark country roads without streetlights, the cabbie was traveling unusually slowly, which is fortunate because he was able to ease off on the gas as he tried to negotiate the taxi around the buck. Each time the taxi moved, so did the deer, bumping into the door and window next to me. We finally moved around it and entered the driveway, leaving the animal still standing in the center of the road. I laughed to myself about the irony of the situation. I had just spent several weeks surrounded by lions, elephants, buffalo, antelope, and assorted other African wildlife, only to have my closest encounter with an animal almost on my very doorstep.

Considering that humans in a vehicle are shielded by steel, aluminum, or plastic, it would seem that they should suffer less collision damage than an unprotected deer, which typically weighs between one hundred and three hundred pounds. It is often not so, perhaps because deer routinely end up going through the windshield. A nonscientific survey of accident accounts suggests that the worst results, often fatalities, occur when impact sends a deer through the windshield and onto people in the vehicle's front seat.

A Lorain, Ohio, man died in November 2012 after his truck hit a trophy-size, 250-pound twelve-point buck, which crashed fully through the windshield and lodged in the cab.

In May 2013, a Washington County, Indiana, driver died instantly when a car in the opposite lane launched a deer airborne, sending it flying through the windshield of the victim's oncoming truck. A similar accident in February 2012 killed a passenger in a car on a West Virginia highway. Even a fragment of a deer can become a lethal projectile if it blasts through a windshield. A seventy-year-old female motorist died after she was hit by the head of a deer that crashed through the windshield of her car after being severed by another vehicle.

The incidence of highway accidents involving deer peaks during the fall breeding season, from about October to December, especially during morning and evening commutes when visibility may be poor and deer are more active. Their sexual and territorial juices flowing, deer are agitated and active, dispersing, on the move, and unpredictable. With mating on their mind they are much more likely to dart into roads heedlessly, especially in the case of a buck focused on a doe. They may suddenly stop in the middle of a road, crossing and even recrossing it.

The mating urge is triggered by shorter days and cooler weather. Deer are especially active at dawn and dusk, which in many states coincides with peak commuting hours when standard time takes over in the fall. The combination means that drivers are more numerous and deer more active when light is low at dusk or glare from the morning sun is worst.

Accidents with deer show no signs of decreasing, and seem guaranteed to continue rising. A study by State Farm in 2009 indicated that in five years the rate of deer-vehicle accidents had gone up 18.3 percent. A reason for the increase was cited in the October 24, 2012, edition of the trade publication *Insurance Journal.* "An increase in urban sprawl and more roads being built through wildlife habitats have displaced deer from their natural habitat, leading to a rise in deer-vehicle collisions, according to the Insurance Information Institute." The institute, an industry organization, is only partly correct. Urban sprawl is partly to blame, but it is off-target to conclude that displacement of deer from their natural habitat is the problem. To the contrary, urban—or, more precisely, suburban—sprawl has actually created more deer habitat.

The suburban patchwork of lawns, gardens, parks, cemeteries, golf courses, playing fields, and leftover patches of woodland is a paradise for deer. An "edge city" is so called not because it is on the edge of an urban area, as the term is most commonly applied, but because it contains so much edge habitat. The density of houses and the antigun mentality of many suburban residents and governing bodies severely restrict or even eliminate sport hunting, the main control over deer populations. Typical is wealthy Westchester County, north of the Bronx and New York City's original suburb. Leafy and bucolic, with northern reaches still described as "the country" by some urbanites overly conditioned to concrete, much of Westchester seems the picture of pastorality. You will not find any licensed deer hunters in those woods with a shotgun or rifle cradled underarm. Law allows only the bow. Neither city nor country, suburbs like Westchester may look semirural, but ruled by urban mentality and mores. They are the ultimate safe haven for deer.

As a result, the concentration of deer in suburban areas now often far exceeds those in the outlands. I see the difference regularly. In 1972, I moved from Fairfield, Connecticut, in the county of the same name, to a more woodsy community fifty miles east, because the last place I could shoot—and usually miss—ruffed grouse had been converted to a golf course. It was clear to me that putters had become preferred over shotguns, and people like me had become an endangered species in town. Fairfield County, with its towns of Greenwich, Darien, and New Canaan, is a towering example of a suburb with an obscene amount of deer. Some parts of the county have a hundred deer per acre, five times the state average. Although deer density considered healthy varies according to the specifics of the habitat, woodlands like those in Connecticut can reasonably support between ten and fifteen deer per square mile, the lower end of the range best of all.

The healthy concentration of animals that a given piece of territory can support is referred to as its "biological carrying capacity." Cultural carrying capacity, defined as the maximum number of deer people can tolerate around them, will be discussed later. In the long run, its importance may trump even that of biology. Dear easily exceed carrying capacity because they reproduce exponentially. A 2009 report of the Northeast Deer Technical Committee referred to a study at the George Reserve in southern Michigan, which tracked a herd that grew from 10 to 212 deer in five years. Does are fawn factories, churning out ten to twelve young during the ten to twelve years of their reproductive lives, which is an adaptive response to high losses from predation when nature is in balance. Where nature is imbalanced in favor of deer, sport hunters replace predators. Where neither control is available, deer far exceed the carrying capacity.

As a result, deer literally eat themselves out of house and home, and quickly—one deer can consume a ton and a half of vegetation in a year. Standing on their hind legs if necessary, they strip the understory to a height of seven feet. They devour tree seedlings and the shoots of young grasses, and munch on herbaceous plants. Eventually they can diminish the diversity of a forest community from top to bottom. Deer may not be able to reach the treetops, but by consuming seedlings, trees have no chance to grow in the first place. Thus, trees that die or cut are not replaced. By eating acorns and oak seedlings, as well as sugar maple seedlings, deer have

changed productive woodlands into those dominated by less valuable species such as American beech and striped maple. Vegetation on the ground often consists only of plants deer find unpalatable, such as some of the scented ferns and a few sedges and grasses. Canada yews, which deer relish, are declining in the northeastern states. So is the herbaceous plant trillium.

Vegetation loss starts the vicious cycle of erosion, leading to more vegetation loss. Eventually, the habitat no longer exists in its original form. Before that point, starvation and disease often decimate the deer herds in a way that, unlike managed culling, compromises their return to health. When I drive through the aforesaid Fairfield County and see deer by the roadside, they are generally scraggly and scrawny, nowhere near as large as those that show up daily outside my home. Other animals suffer as well. Loss of understory eliminates birds that nest on the ground, and others, such as many warblers, that enjoy the brush. Nestlings and eggs of birds that nest on the ground or near it are more vulnerable to predators once cover is stripped away.

The damage caused by deer to the timber industry totals more than $750 million annually, according to figures cited by the Cornell University Cooperative Extension Wildlife Damage Management Program. The toll on farm crops is about $200 million. Homeowners lose $250 million of garden and landscaping plants to deer each year, a conservative estimate.

Many people no longer plant tulips because deer are especially attracted to the bulbs. A woman who had just moved to the area asked a landscaper I know to plant about a thousand dollars' worth of tulips in her yard. He explained to her that it was a bad idea, given local precedent. She insisted. When not a tulip emerged the following spring, she badgered the landscaper for her money back, unsuccessfully. Based on what he had told her, she could not plead ignorance.

I have waged battle against hungry deer for years on the borders of the large vegetable garden I maintain for my household and a small vegetable stand. The stand loses money, but people in the area enjoy it, so I keep it open. In the spring, literally the morning after I till, the newly turned soil is covered with the prints of deer hooves, as if they are already checking out the garden's prospects and drooling over the feast to come. After years of trying all sorts of tactics to keep them out—to be discussed later in the chapter—I found that only one works. Electric fencing keeps them away. Most of the time, that is.

There is no better example of how hungry deer can cause a thunderous ruckus among homeowners, municipal officials, and an entire community than in the appropriately named city of Town and Country. Incorporated in 1950, it is the consummate suburb, the perfect setting for wildlife looking to set up house in an urban realm. Twelve miles from St. Louis, Missouri, it is home to eleven thousand people and one of the nation's wealthiest communities, right up there with Greenwich, Connecticut. The city's website describes it as a "presti-gious suburban community" with "generous, well-landscaped lots," where "the original country charm of larger lots with white fences and grazing horses still can be found." More-over, "several large tracts of land . . . remain undeveloped" making it a "quiet, restful, green residential area." And one where contentious debates over what to do about its up to sixty deer per square mile have made headlines since the 1990s. Issued in January 2013, the 2012 report of the city's deer-management program noted that some residents con-tinue to feed deer, making efforts to control them more diffi-cult. After decades of effort, the town still has an overabun-dance of deer in many neighborhoods, and some homeowners continue to feed them. That overabundance not only wreaks havoc on landscaping. Deer caused seventy-eight accidents in the city during 2010.

Just as deer trickled from the wilderness into the suburbs, the burbs are wellsprings from which deer seep into big cities. Virtually every large city in the land has its errant deer, and some even have resident populations. In 2010, a doe penetrated downtown St. Louis, where it banged into a store window and later was found dead. In 2009, cars screeched to a halt and pedestrians scattered as a young deer raced through the streets of downtown Savannah, Georgia. With the police literally on its tail, it scampered through the heart of town until it was darted with a tranquilizer gun in an attempt, unsuccessful, to save it. New York's Finest made news several times chasing deer instead of muggers around the Bronx. One incident drew chuckles from television viewers, as police officers, obviously uncomfortable in their role as temporary game wardens, cluelessly attempted to corral two of the animals. Another borough of New York City, Staten Island, has its own deer herd of several dozen. Deer probably reached the borough by swimming across the narrow waters of Arthur Kill from New Jersey.

In 2006, downtown Cincinnati was visited by a deer that crashed through a window into a hotel and trashed the lobby before it was euthanized. Deer that wander into town have a penchant for entering buildings. A doe and two fawns took advantage of the automatic doors to enter and exit a Kohl's department store in Coralville, Iowa. Customers in a Niagara Falls, New York, grocery store dove for cover as a deer wandered in through the door, then crashed through a glass window to exit. In February 2012 in a Houston, Texas, neighborhood, authorities had to euthanize deer in two different homes on the same day, after the animals crashed through windows and turned several rooms upside down. In the same month, a year before, a deer entered the home of a Newburyport, Massachusetts, woman and, overturning the tables, frightened her dog. Police tranquilized and removed the deer.

Deer incidents can be quite amusing. In June 2013, a deer from nearby woods ran onto the track at the Keeneland Racecourse in Lexington, Kentucky, sixty miles east of Churchill Downs. It attempted to keep pace with a pair of horses, prompting quips in the media about the animal showing up too late for the Kentucky Derby.

But there is nothing funny about another aspect of deer proliferation: its role in the spread of Lyme disease. Lyme disease is caused by *Borrelia burgdorferi,* a whip-tailed bacterium called a spirochete. Lyme disease has so many symptoms it has been called the "great imitator." Often accompanied by a bull's-eye-shaped red rash, early on it triggers fatigue, chills, fever, muscle and joint pain, and a host of unpleasant aftereffects. Increasingly, evidence shows it can be chronic if not treated in time, and even threaten life.

Deer are the main host for the adult stage-two ticks

spread the disease, the deer tick or black-legged tick (*Ioxodes scapularis*) in the eastern part of the country and the western black-legged tick (*I. pacificus*) in the West. The darkest areas on maps that illustrate deer density match those on maps depicting the highest incidence of Lyme disease, notably the Middle Atlantic and northeastern states and those of the upper Midwest. Studies indicate that as deer populations rise, so do cases of Lyme disease. Fairfield County, with Connecticut's highest deer density, also ranks highest for Lyme disease, in a state that usually is first or second in the nation for the most cases.

The true magnitude of Lyme disease as a public health crisis was revealed in July 2013 when, at a conference on the disease in Boston, the federal Centers for Disease Control (CDC) finally admitted what Lyme activists had been saying for years. The incidence of Lyme disease was vastly understated by the agency, which had considered only cases meeting a rigid set of criteria as reportable. "We know that routine surveillance only gives us part of the picture, and that the true number of illnesses is much greater," said Paul Mead, chief of epidemiology and surveillance for CDC's Lyme disease program, quoted in an August 19, 2013, CDC press release. "This new preliminary estimate confirms that Lyme disease is a tremendous public health problem in the United States, and clearly highlights the urgent need for prevention."

"Much greater" indeed. The increase was by a factor of ten, from thirty thousand cases to three hundred thousand cases a year.

Additionally, Lyme ticks can infect the victim with at least three other diseases, conceivably, but not usually, with one bite. The fever and malaise symptoms of babesiosis, anaplasmosis, and ehrlichiosis all resemble one another and Lyme disease as well. Because the entire batch of them is caused by bacteria, antibiotics are effective against one and all.

I learned about Lyme disease the hard way, having been treated for it five times over the past three decades. My family physician is a recognized authority on treating the disease and was among the first to recognize how severe it can become. Lyme disease is a focal point for me in many ways.

It is named for the wooded town where it was first identified in 1975, Lyme, just across the Connecticut River from where I live. (We now know that the disease has actually been around since prehistory but not recognized as such.) At the time the disease was identified, I regularly hunted a piece of property in Lyme. My own town, Killingworth, has been the site of key research on deer ticks; arguably the world's foremost expert on Lyme ticks lives about a half mile from me. I have written about Lyme disease in a host of magazines, including *Audubon* and *Field & Stream*. My writing has been utilized by organizations to explain the disease to lay people. I knew some of the first people to be certified as infected. I quoted one of them in an article I wrote for *Field & Stream* in May 1985: "I felt totally weak and useless," he said. He added that his chest itched and his head ached for three months. Periodically, in the first three years after the disease was diagnosed, his knee and elbow joints swelled painfully for weeks at a time.

Between then and now, it is not an exaggeration to say that a majority of my outdoor friends have contracted tick-borne illnesses. So have many of our gun dogs. When one good friend has a tick bite, he pops antibiotics given to him for his dogs. In my neck of the woods, where many people spend considerable time afield recreating, cutting wood, or working the soil, Lyme disease has become a routine fact of life. Few people panic over a tick bite. Not so in urban communities. In July 2013, a New York City–based writer who summers on Block Island, off the Rhode Island coast, expressed the horror that urbanites have for the tiny arachnid that is the tick. "I'm consumed by fear along with many other parents on the island. I examine my children several times a day," Hope Reeves wrote in the *New York Times* blog *Motherlode* (July 12, 2013). For people whose outdoor experience consists largely of playing in parks, thickets and woodlands are places to be avoided. Something scary lurks out there, even in the bushes at the edge of the lawn. The specter so feared is no bigger than the period at the end of this sentence. Around my way, if we see a tick on our body, we pick it off and torch it with a match. Or flush it down the toilet. The good ole boys from the rod and gun club, the hard-core birders, the backpackers, do not let the bogeyman of Lyme disease keep them out of the woods. Instead of quivering in dread, they stay aware of the problem and handle it if they need to do so. And that's that.

A side note from history: Of that tick, in 1754, Swedish naturalist Pehr Kalm wrote prophetically on return from a three-year study of natural history in America published in *Memoirs of the Swedish Academy of Science*: "This small vile creature may, in the future, cause the inhabitants of this land great damage unless a method is discovered which will prevent it from increasing at such a shocking rate." He made this observation while in the Hudson River valley, where deer were already decreasing. Had he only known.

Some potential dangers that deer pose may escape notice due to the fact that these creatures are often thought of as victims rather than agressors. Does will sometimes react to perceived threats to their young by utilizing their extremely sharp hooves. Clay K. Nielsen, the same scientist who led the groundbreaking study of cougar expansion discussed earlier, coauthored a paper on whitetail does attacking thirteen people on the campus of Southern Illinois University at Carbondale during the fawning seasons of 2005 and 2006.

"Wildlife managers may face the increased likelihood of

aggressive behavior from deer directed towards humans as deer and human populations increase and come into closer contact with each other," the paper maintained.

The modus operandi of the attackers was to stand upright on rear legs and flail at the target with front hooves. The injuries sustained by the victims ranged from minor scrapes to a broken collarbone. One of the victims, a police officer, responded by shooting his attacker with his sidearm. The others usually ran away. Nielsen and his colleague, wildlife researcher Ryan D. Hubbard, note that the areas in which the attacks took place were near wooded corridors, where fawns could hide while their mothers browsed. So all three elements necessary for the attack were there—the doe, the fawn or fawns, and humans. Deer on the campus were accustomed to people who were not a threat to them, thus without fear, another factor the researchers figured might have contributed to the attacks.

As for the implications of the attacks, the researchers issued a warning. "As human populations increase in areas of high-quality deer habitat and as deer populations grow where hunting is restricted or prohibited, deer attacks could increase." They added a dire footnote, acknowledging that "such attacks can be . . . deadly to humans." Children, they said, are especially at risk, given that they lack the size and strength to defend themselves. Parents and officials who manage playgrounds, parks, and athletic fields that abut wooded areas would do well to ponder Hubbard and Nielsen's research.

The danger to life and limb from attacks by deer—not to mention highway accidents—pales in comparison to what happens if the aggressor is a moose. In Alaska, where moose are especially common, the state Department of Fish and Game warns that more people are injured by moose attacks than those by bears. Crashing a vehicle into one of these massive creatures—six feet tall at the shoulder and weighing up to sixteen hundred pounds—is like running into reinforced concrete. Typically, when an automobile hits a moose, the hood strikes the animal's long legs and the massive body tumbles onto the car or windshield. Connecticut's Wildlife Division, alerting the public to the new danger of moose on the highways in that state, cites accident statistics collected from states where the animals are common. It suggests that vehicular collisions with moose are thirty times more likely to result in a human death than those with deer. Hit a moose and there is a one in fifty chance you will not come out of it alive, according to the Connecticut handout.

Until relatively recently, collisions with moose were likely only in Alaska, with about six hundred per year, and northern New England, especially Maine, which averages about seven hundred accidents annually. The toll probably would be higher if these areas had human populations with densities comparable to those of more urbanized states. Moose, however, are on the move, in a recovery that is bringing them into urban fringes. "Even greater testimony to the parallel growth of human and moose populations is the increased incidents of moose wandering into the suburban and urban areas of Spokane," notes the Washington Department of Fish and Wildlife on its website. Historically moose retreated north and up into mountains from their historical range, which stretched as far south as northern Colorado, southern New England, and northern Pennsylvania.

A signal that times were changing occurred in June 1998, when a married couple was injured when their car hit a female moose on traffic-clogged Interstate 95, in Old Saybrook, Connecticut. Prior to that, the idea of a moose trotting across a highway corridor between New York City and Boston and a few miles from Long Island Sound was beyond belief. Within a decade, however, at least a hundred moose, probably more, inhabited Connecticut and had begun reproducing there. The hitherto unthinkable reality of moose wandering Connecticut stems from a dramatic increase in moose populations in Maine, New Hampshire, and Vermont during the 1980s and 1990s. Moose populations recovered in the North due to better management and, importantly, the regrowth of hardwoods over clear-cuts. Moose need browse consisting of leaves and twigs from woody plants such as aspen, birch, maple, and mountain ash. Out West, Washington's moose population has grown from zero into the 1950s to about one thousand animals. From Washington, as well as Idaho, moose are edging into Oregon, the first in modern times. Moose began entering New York State in the 1980s, and now approach a thousand in number.

During 2013, a decline in moose populations in New Hampshire and Minnesota garnered headlines in the media. Scientists pointed to an increase in blood-sucking ticks, which cause anemia in moose, and other parasites. The increase in pests was attributed to a warming climate. The increase in moose south of their main range, however, leaves the climate question up in the air. Additionally, moose populations in Minnesota have gone through bust periods in the past, then boomed again. Moose populations seem to be expanding in many other parts of their range. Utah has so many moose that in 2007 it traded a couple of dozen female moose to Colorado for approximately an equal amount of bighorn sheep.

A 2006 study led by Justin D. Hoffman of the University of Nebraska documented the long-distance dispersal of moose in the central United States after populations increased in Minnesota and North Dakota. The study traced moose traveling as far south as the Texas Panhandle and Missouri. The travelers, suggested Hoffman and his colleagues, are not footloose wanderers or animals stricken by a brain parasite, as sometimes theorized, but "founder individuals that are dispersing naturally from established populations in search of suitable habitats and mates in areas to the south." They also suggested that moose are repeating expansion from north to south that occurred when they arrived from Asia via the Bering land bridge, along with human colonists at the end of the ice ages. Their findings, they added, should prompt wildlife managers to gear up for dealing with moose in habitats far to the south of where they live now. It is difficult to envision, but if they are right, I BRAKE FOR MOOSE stickers could become as common on bumpers in Kansas and Nebraska as they are in Maine.

Here are just a few fatal accidents involving moose:

A Williamstown, Vermont, man died after his pickup truck smashed into a moose on Interstate 89 while he was on his way to work. The accident occurred a short while before dawn. The moose died as well.

In October 2008, a female driver died when her car hit a moose in Sanbornton, New Hampshire, on Interstate 93, leading to Boston, and rolled over. She was killed on impact.

In September 2012, a Canadian man slammed into a moose on a highway in Dennistown, Maine. He was thrown from his vehicle and found dead by a motorist.

Not unexpectedly, most smashups with moose take place between dawn and dusk. Why did the moose cross the road? Not just to get from one side to the other. Moose come to roadways for many reasons. During the summer, the open road is airy, with the breeze sweeping away flies that pester the animals. Spring brings them to the roadside to feed on emerging vegetation after the cold winter. In Maine and elsewhere, May and June are peak times for accidents with moose.

During winter, moose take advantage of easier going provided by plowed roads—and snowmobile trails—when snow is deep in the woods. They also consume road salt for its sodium. Moose require a high level of sodium. When lakes and ponds are ice-free, they get it from eating aquatic plants. Lacking those, they may consume what the salt trucks leave behind.

After a series of moose attacks on people in Alaska during the spring of 2011, a biologist for the state was quoted by the *Huffington Post* as advising residents who encounter the animals to "assume every moose is a serial killer standing in the middle of the trail with a loaded gun" (May 27, 2011). He obviously exaggerated to make a point, but it was well taken. Moose can kill and often turn aggressive any time, but they are especially nasty in late spring and early summer, when cows are protective of young calves. During spring and early summer 2012, Alaska experienced a spate of moose attacks by females with young. Three occurred not in the wilds but in Anchorage, the state's largest city: a girl on a bicycle was battered, a boy knocked unconscious, and a woman kicked. The other attack occurred forty miles from Anchorage, in Palmer. It was the most serious. A cow moose thundered into a woman from behind, knocked her down, repeatedly stomped her, and then bolted for the woods. When state troopers arrived, the moose charged them. They were forced to shoot, and killed the animal. A moose with a calf kicked a woman who was walking four dogs in Missoula, Montana, in May 2013. The presence of dogs made matters worse, because moose equate them with marauding wolves. Chances of attack in such a case are extremely high. Bulls during fall mating season are bristling for a battle, be it with other male moose or people who cross their path. Like humans, they get the winter blues. A moose tired from wading through deep snow can be exceedingly irritable. A moose that is sick or injured may also turn mean. Authorities suspect this is why a moose attacked a ninety-two-year-old man who was walking to church in the village of Grand Lake, Colorado, in March 2006. After authorities killed the moose, they found it had broken ribs and spinal damage, probably from a collision with a vehicle.

Safety Tips: Moose and Deer

State wildlife agencies in states with moose populations generally agree on how to avoid confrontations with them. First and foremost, give them plenty of space. Never try to feed them, something that, weird as it may seem, people occasionally attempt. If hiking and you see a moose on the trail, yield the way. If you encounter a cow in spring and early summer, back off immediately. Odds are she is not alone and a calf is nearby. Make sure you do not get between mother and offspring. If a moose wanders into a suburban or urban neighborhood, contact authorities and stay away. Keep children and dogs inside. A moose may feel cornered in a congested area and panic.

As the Washington Department of Fish and Wildlife cautions on its website, "A moose that sees you and walks slowly towards you is not trying to be your friend." Its body language is warning you to back off. If it lays back its hairs, the hair on its shoulder hump stands up, and it swings its head and stops, it is very edgy. If you are close enough to see it licking its lips, get away quickly. It is not relishing you as a meal, but the results could be just as disastrous. Many charges by moose turn out to be bluffs, but most experts suggest that you run. Since the moose is not a predator like cougars or bears, running does not trigger a prey response. A moose just wants to run you off; typically it will not chase very far and it is not nearly as fleet as it looks.

If the worst happens and the moose knocks you down, take the standard approach when a big animal has you on the ropes. Curl up in a ball, protecting your head with your arms and hands. And pray that you are not about to be stomped to jelly.

Advice on avoiding collisions with deer hold for moose as well. If you see a deer near the highway, slow down and watch for sudden movement. If the deer is in the road and does not move out of the way, do not try to steer around it. Consider the experience described above when a buck continued to bump into my taxi. Wait for the deer to pass and the road is clear. DEER CROSSING signs are there for a reason. Slow down when traveling through areas known to have a high concentration of deer so you will have ample time to stop if necessary.

If you are traveling after dark, use high beams when there is no oncoming traffic. High beams will be reflected by the eyes of deer on or near roads. If you see one deer, be on guard: others may be in the area. Deer in family groups cross roads single-file. If a collision appears inevitable, do not swerve to avoid impact. Brake firmly, but stay in your lane. The choice is unpleasant, but hitting the deer is probably less likely to be fatal than swerving and hitting oncoming traffic or a tree.

As far as Lyme disease is concerned, you will not contract it unless a tick carrying the spirochete bites you and hangs on for twenty-four hours. The Centers for Disease Control has advice for preventing tick bites. It is sound, but I believe it is extreme. If I followed it, I would spend more time dealing with ticks than I do in activities that expose me to them— and these are activities I love. In fact, I would not be able to successfully hunt or freshwater fish or even undertake serious birding. I might be able to hike, but only on manicured trails. It is the kind of public information that terrifies people into putting HAZMAT suits on their kids when they go out to play.

Nevertheless, here is the CDC's advice, as found on its website:

PREVENTING TICK BITES

While it is a good idea to take preventive measures against ticks year-round, be extra vigilant in warmer months (April–September) when ticks are most active.

- Avoid Direct Contact with Ticks. Avoid wooded and bushy areas with high grass and leaf litter. Walk in the center of trails. Repel Ticks with DEET or Permethrin
- Use repellents that contain 20% to 30% DEET (N, N diethyl-m-toluamide) on exposed skin and clothing for protection that lasts up to several hours. Always follow product instructions. Parents should apply this product to their children, avoiding hands, eyes, and mouth.
- Use products that contain permethrin on clothing. Treat clothing and gear, such as boots, pants, socks and tents. It remains protective through several washings. Pre-treated clothing is available and remains protective for up to 70 washings.
- Other repellents registered by the Environmental Protection Agency (EPA) may be found at http://cfpub.epa.gov/opref/insect/.

FIND AND REMOVE TICKS FROM YOUR BODY

- Bathe or shower as soon as possible after coming indoors (preferably within two hours) to wash off and more easily find ticks that are crawling on you.
- Conduct a full-body tick check using a hand-held or full-length mirror to view all parts of your body upon return from tick-infested areas. Parents should check

their children for ticks under the arms, in and around the ears, inside the belly button, behind the knees, between the legs, around the waist, and especially in their hair.

- Examine gear and pets. Ticks can ride into the home on clothing and pets, then attach to a person later, so carefully examine pets, coats, and day packs.
- Tumble clothes in a dryer on high heat for an hour to kill remaining ticks.

TIPS FOR DEER-FREE GARDENING

Of all the problems caused by deer, preventing them from using flower beds, shrubbery, and vegetables as a cafeteria is the most difficult to solve. I am a master gardener, with a certification from the University of Connecticut Cooperative Extension System hanging on my office wall. Over the years, I have tried as many different ways of keeping deer out of my vegetable garden as I could find. I researched, talked to landscapers, and visited garden shops. I experimented with clear fishing line and Irish Spring soap. Unlike the pretty lady in the television advertisement who said of the soap's scent, "Manly, yes, but I like it, too," deer were supposed to be put off by the aroma. I even wrote so in a major hook-and-bullet magazine. I hung bars of the soap on stakes in my garden. It worked. That is, until the deer became accustomed to the smell. They also grow accustomed to many so-called repellents, many of which cannot be used on fruits and vegetables. The Texas Cooperative Extension Service produced an excellent assessment, *Gardening in Deer Country*. Its advice on repellents is this: "Repellents may be somewhat effective for a period of time if the population density of deer is low and there is enough alternative foliage for them to consume." The deer in my yard also learned quickly that clear fishing line fenced around the garden was not a puzzling invisible barrier but something that could be easily traversed. Deer are smart and soon learn when they are not in true danger.

I finally decided that I needed electric fencing, bit the bullet and purchased a form of electric netting that is used in the United Kingdom, which has its own deer problems. It has worked, most of the time. There are alternatives to fences that zap. Many types of fencing and netting will keep deer out of gardens. The catch is that for a garden of moderate size, the barrier must be at least eight feet high and preferably a few feet higher than that. A lower fence works only if the garden is so small the deer feel that they do not have enough room to jump back over it.

Many homeowners who want deer-free landscaping try to find plants that deer do not readily consume, which is not so easy, because deer have such an indiscriminate diet—they'll readily nibble poison ivy. Many landscapers and nurseries sell plants they describe as "deer proof." Some of them are, until a shortage of other plants forces deer to sample anything available. Prickly pear, for example, is sometimes sold as a plant deer avoid. They may, unless they need moisture. Scented ferns, like maidenhair and wood fern, generally grow unmolested by deer, but again, not if these are the only plants around to assuage hunger pangs. The best advice I can find for homeowners who worry about deer eating their landscaping is from the Cornell Cooperative Extension Wildlife Damage Management Program, in its fact sheet on white-tailed deer: "No plants are completely deer proof, and hungry deer will consume plants that have little nutritional value."

In the long run, there is no surefire solution.

CHAPTER 7

GATORS ON THE GOLF COURSE:
Will Success Spoil the American Alligator?

If you live in the South and a twelve-foot American alligator is paddling around your pool or basking by your barbecue, you can blame me. During the late 1960s, when I was a curator at the New York Zoological Society, I was assigned as a representative to an organization called the American Alligator Council. I served with state and federal wildlife biologists, other zoo curators, wildlife law enforcement officers, alligator farmers, and, I suspect, one or two former gator poachers reborn as conservationists. Our goal was to help state wildlife agencies develop recovery programs for the American alligator, which the U.S. Fish and Wildlife Service had declared an endangered species in 1967.

During the late 1960s, we observed populations of alligators in many different habitats from one end of the range map to the other. We watched gators glide among the floating peat islands of the Okefenokee Swamp. We checked alligator nests in the sawgrass prairies of Florida's Everglades. We observed the surrealistic sight of alligators, little changed from their Mesozoic ancestors, basking on mud banks at the Kennedy Space Center, in the shadow of the massive assembly building where the Apollo/Saturn vehicles were put together before rocketing spaceward. In the Florida Panhandle, we tracked alligators along the sinuous bends of the Apalachicola River winding through the national forest of the same name. From the long, flat ridges, or cheniers, rising above the marshes of Cameron Parish on Louisiana's border with Texas, we watched gators in the state-owned Rockefeller Refuge, where wildlife coexisted quite compatibly with functioning oil rigs.

At the time, only forty thousand alligators remained in Louisiana. By 1972, Cameron Parish alone had so many alligators that the state opened a thirteen-day hunting season there, eventually expanded statewide by 1981 as the alligator population increased and spread out. The explosive growth of Louisiana's alligator population reflects what happened throughout alligator territory. Few wildlife-conservation efforts have met such rapid and massive success as the restoration to abundance—indeed, superabundance—of the American alligator. Within twenty years of the species being declared endangered, southern states were knee-deep in alligators. The thunderous bellows of gators seeking mates boomed in the night from coastal North Carolina to the Rio Grande in Texas. By the beginning of the twenty-first century, approximately five million gators—two million in Louisiana and more than a million in Florida alone—were swimming in waters of ten states. Concurrently, the southeastern states experienced a huge influx of humans migrating to the burgeoning urban areas and retirement communities of the Sun Belt. The population of Florida alone more than doubled from 1970 to a total of almost sixteen million in 2000, according to the United States Census. It is not an exaggeration to say that the use of air conditioning has brought millions of people within reach of alligator jaws.

Those jaws are of ancient design. To quote the website of the theme park and entertainment giant SeaWorld Parks & Entertainment: "Alligators are one animal that has changed very little since the prehistoric days." Alligators, along with all crocodilians, belong to a group of reptiles known as the archosaurs, the ruling reptiles (from *archon,* Greek for ruler, and *sauros,* Greek for lizard). Other major groups of animals that arose from the archosaurs include the dinosaurs and, biologist now recognize, birds. Along with its primitive appearance, by anyone's measure the alligator is an exceedingly large as well as primeval beast. Many adult males approach fourteen feet long and one thousand pounds in weight. They can get even bigger, approaching twenty feet, equaling some of the biggest crocodiles in size. Socketed in their jaws are eighty or so replaceable teeth, all of them cone-shaped and without differentiation as in mammals. Development of socketed teeth by the ancestors of crocodilians and dinosaurs was a major step up on the evolutionary ladder.

Some truly giant Mesozoic crocodilians apparently preyed on dinosaurs. Among them was *Sarcosuchus imperator,* a crocodilian forty feet long and weighing up to eighteen thousand pounds, with six-foot jaws. This bus-sized prehistoric crocodile probably lurked at the water's edge and grabbed small dinosaurs when they came to drink or feed on water plants. It is not difficult to imagine an alligator considering using its socketed teeth on a human at water's edge; to *Sarcosuchus* we'd be viewed as a small bipedal dinosaur that might make a decent meal. Alligators do not immediately home in on humans as prey, the way many crocodiles do. Still, they kill people, and attacks of all kinds, both predatory and defensive, are increasing as gator and human share living space. Whether familiarization with people will increase attacks even more is uncertain but probable. Especially in the water, a hungry alligator is unlikely to give a human a pass if the opportunity for an easy meal presents itself. Dogs and cats? For alligators, they are munchies.

In the wild, alligators eat virtually anything that moves, and often things that do not, in the form of carrion. Young alligators snap up fish, insects, snails, crustaceans, and worms. As they grow in size, so does the bulk of the animals they choose as prey. Larger gators graduate to eating turtles, wading and water birds, deer, raccoons, otters, feral pigs, and even an occasional Florida panther, a subspecies of cougar.

The jaws of the alligator are adapted to crush and grip prey, and they close with enormous force. In 2002, a Florida State University biology professor, Greg Erickson, conducted an experiment at the St. Augustine Alligator Farm Zoological Park that registered the bite of alligators with a measuring device at the end of an engineered pole, seven feet long. The device consisted of metal "bite bars" resembling large tuning forks. The bars, which were covered in leather to prevent damage to the alligators' teeth, contained strain gauges that measure force. Not surprisingly, the bigger the alligator, the harder the bite. A 665-pound alligator, twelve feet long, bit down with a force of 2,125 pounds. Erickson equated the effort it would take to escape from the creature's jaws to lifting a small pickup truck. In comparison, a lion has a bite force of about 940 pounds. The bone-crushing bite of a hyena is about 1,000 pounds. The dusky shark achieves about 330 pounds.

While the muscles that enable alligator jaws to snap shut with crushing power are exceptionally strong, those that open the mouth are relatively weak. This is the secret of why alligator wrestlers can hold a gator's jaws closed with one hand. The uniform dentition of the crocodilians is not built for chewing but for crushing, gripping, and ripping off pieces of flesh. They dispatch small prey, then gulp it down whole. Alligators often kill larger animals by holding them underwater to drown. Medium-sized prey or big pieces of meat are manipulated around in the mouth until positioned to swallow. If a victim is too large to swallow, the alligator performs a "death roll." It grabs a mouthful of flesh or an appendage and then spins round and round amid a cloud of bubbles and swirling water until the piece detaches from the body. A scientific study showed that during the roll, the alligator rotates on the longitudinal axis of its body powered by flexing and canting its head and tail.

Lazing in the sun, an alligator looks sluggish and slow moving. Far from it. When need be, an alligator moves with surprising speed, in and out of the water. While tales of alligators swimming at thirty miles an hour are balderdash, even though repeated regularly on the Web, alligators can cruise at close to ten miles an hour. Unlike almost all other reptiles, crocodilians can raise themselves on their legs and thus move with surprising speed on the ground. Alligators can launch themselves into short overland bursts of up to nine miles an hour.

Alligators and their relatives also lunge explosively. I once had a two-foot caiman, a close tropical American cousin of the alligator, in my bathtub. (At one time in my life, people who became tired of their exotic pets often deposited them with me for transfer to zoos.) From the floor of the tub, where it was resting, it lunged up and over the rim like a scaly rocket and nailed me on the arm with its teeth. To get at me, the creature covered a distance longer than its own length in a single burst. It is that speed than makes the alligator and its kin effective ambush predators, lying in wait by the waterside for an unwary animal to approach.

What you have in the American alligator is a prehistoric eating machine, a flesh-and-blood Godzilla, minus the fiery breath, a prehistoric survivor ensconced by the millions among gated communities, schools, shopping centers, golf courses, and parks of uptown and downtown inhabited by like numbers of people. In October 2013, a six-foot gator ambled near the automatic sliding door of a Wal-Mart supercenter store in Apopka, Florida. As customers scattered, while the door opened and closed, employees initiated a lockdown. The

gator finally left for nearby woods, and was later captured by authorities. As far as humans interacting with alligators are concerned, Florida is the epicenter. The Sunshine State has all the elements that create conflict between people and alligators, and it has them to the max. Florida has a corner on confrontations with the reptiles, ranging from alligators making a nuisance of themselves to alligators killing people. No one has ever been killed by an alligator in Texas. One person has been killed in Georgia, a woman attacked and eaten by an eight-foot gator in a swanky housing development near Savannah. But, by and large, hardly anyone gets killed by alligators outside Florida. Since record-keeping began in 1948, twenty-two people have died there in the jaws of alligators, according to the latest figures from the state's Fish and Wildlife Conservation Commission. During that same period, more than three hundred unprovoked attacks have occurred, about five per year. Reports of alligators that are scaring people or just making a pest of themselves—"nuisance alligators"—number about sixteen thousand a year.

Contrast those figures with statistics from Louisiana, which has even more alligators than Florida but much fewer people, less than five million. Louisiana wildlife authorities receive less than a quarter as many nuisance alligator reports as Florida, and it is not because alligators are better behaved there. As far as anyone knows, no one has been killed by an alligator in Louisiana. You can count the number of recorded attacks on the fingers of your two hands and probably have a digit or two left over. Attacks do seem to be increasing, ever so slightly, which may not be surprising given that the state's population has risen almost 50 percent since 2000. By and large, however, alligator attacks are a rarity in the land of poboys and jambalaya.

"The historically low attack rate in Louisiana is attributed to a history of intense hunting"—this from a 2005 paper on alligator damage control by two biologists for the State of Florida, Allan R. Woodward and Dennis N. David. They are correct, but only in part. The main reason why people are more likely to be bitten by alligators in Florida than Louisiana, however, may be sociological, having to do with the nature of people themselves. Few areas of the country have a stronger hunting tradition than Louisiana. Large numbers of people, notably members of the Cajun community, but people of other ethnicity as well, live amid the bayous that are prime alligator country. Fishing and hunting are an integral part of their lifestyle. They also turn the tables on alligators. Alligator meat is a delicacy of Cajun cuisine, eaten in about every way imaginable, from barbecued ribs to jambalayas and gumbos.

By contrast, few people—except for outlaws, refugees, and outcasts—have ever lived by choice in the heart of the Everglades or Okefenokee. Certainly, many native Floridians, especially rural types, are accustomed to dealing with alligators. They are in a minority of residents there today. Millions of Florida residents are city slickers from the North, a far cry from Florida swampers or bayou-wise Cajuns who have grown up with gators.

No self-respecting Louisiana Cajun of sound mind and body is going to get nailed by an alligator unless he deliberately risks it. Florida, however, is full of transplants from places like Brooklyn and Des Moines. Until most of them moved south, they never encountered alligators, except perhaps in a zoo. To phrase it nicely, some of them are inclined to act in an unwise fashion around gators. To put it more bluntly, they often place themselves at risk by dumb mistakes such as swimming where alligators lurk or feeding them for fun.

A naive snowbird who is chomped upon while feeding a gator can plead ignorance. It is difficult to imagine the embarrassment when an old Florida hand suffers the same fate, then is charged with a misdemeanor for feeding an alligator. It happened in 2012 when the operator of an airboat tour lost his left hand after trying to lure a gator to the surface of the water for his clients to see.

Although water for drinking, agriculture, and industry is at a premium because of Florida's population growth, development has added immeasurably to the aquatic habitat suitable for alligators. *A Guide to Living with Alligators,* produced by Florida's Fish and Wildlife Conservation Commission, notes that "the growing number of people living and recreating near water has led to a steady rise in the number of alligator-related complaints. . . . Many new residents seek waterfront homes, resulting in increased interactions between people and alligators." Throughout Florida, housing developments, parks, and golf courses are dotted with artificial ponds. More to the point, South Florida, in particular, is laced with so many canals that Venice might seem dry by comparison. It has canals for flood control, irrigation, recreation, navigation, and to provide housing developments with waterfront, which raises the value of real estate. The South Florida Water Management System alone operates twenty-six hundred miles of canals to provide flood control, water supply, navigation, water-quality improvements, and environmental management over its sixteen-county, seventeen-thousand-square-mile region. Its creation was a monumental exercise in civil engineering. Canals range in depth from a few feet to thirty-five feet, plenty of water—and a host of fish ranging from mullet to introduced tropical peacock bass—for alligators. Humans and their technology have created bed and board for alligators so bountiful and welcoming that it is unparalleled as habitat. Perhaps never since crocodilians appeared along with the early dinosaurs, about 250 million years ago, has one of their ilk had it so good.

The irony of a creature that would fit in with the dinosaurs benefiting from modern civil engineering is delicious. The first crocodilians probably were land animals. Some had hind legs much longer than their front legs, indicating they probably were swift runners. Gradually, legs shortened, and many of the crocodilians adapted to aquatic or semiaquatic life, a move that may have saved them from the cataclysm that claimed the dinosaurs.

Long-legged crocodiles were replicated in a SyFi channel movie, *Dinocroc,* about a genetically manipulated monster. SyFi also aired *Supergator,* about an immense bioengineered alligator. The two monsters eventually battled in *Dinocroc vs. Supergator.* Watching the movie, it occurred to me that I had once seen supergators of sorts that were actual byproducts of modern nuclear technology—the stuff of science fiction. While working with the Alligator Council, I visited the Savannah River Plant of the U.S. Atomic Energy Commission, a site in South Carolina that refined nuclear weapons materials. Just as in nuclear power plants, water flushed through the site's reactors acted as a coolant. Spent heated water at Savannah River was cooled in a canal and a reservoir, which spilled over a dam into a second pond. By the time the water reached the second lake, it was cool enough for fish. And for alligators that came there to feed on the fish.

Starting in the 1960s, researchers at the plant's ecology laboratory began to study what happened when the heated waters created unique gradients of water temperature never before experienced by alligators. Big gators there seemed less reliant on the sun's warmth, basking less than usual. Larger males stayed active in the warm waters year round, instead of holing up and lapsing into a winter slowdown typical of alligators in the northern reaches of their range. Food in the form of fish and turtles was also continually available. As a result, the alligators grew more rapidly and reached exceedingly large sizes. Talk about supergators. Filmmakers missed the boat on this one.

The real-life supergators, the outsized Cretaceous crocodilians and giant crocodilians that tended to frequent land, perished with the dinosaurs. The ancestors of today's crocodiles, gavials, caimans, and alligators remained. Perhaps smaller size had something to do with their escape from dinosaur Armageddon. Once the dinosaurs bit the bullet at the end of the Cretaceous period, no prey remained large enough to cure the hunger pangs of the huge crocodilians. Those that survived were species that could manage by eating water animals such as fish. Life in the water in general seems to have weathered the storm that brought down the curtain on the Cretaceous. If any crocodilians remained on land, they could not compete with the mammals that claimed the earth once the reign of the dinosaurs ended, so they disappeared as well.

Most of the crocodilians that survived the Cretaceous were little different in appearance and behavior than modern species. The model that enabled them to survive back then still works, even in habitat shared by a space center. The first true alligators appeared either in North America or Asia almost forty million years ago. Fossils have been found on both continents, and the only other living alligator is the Chinese alligator, much smaller than the American but otherwise a lookalike. Originally, there seems to have been two additional species of alligator in North America. As climate cooled and dried, only the present-day American alligator survived in the warm, moist Southeast.

In places like the Okefenokee and Everglades, the American alligator is what scientists call a keystone species, which means they have profound impact on other species within their wildlife community. As a top predator, they influence the numbers of prey species. They also provide sanctuary for many other species seeking to survive drought. Adult gators dig holes that fill with water and provide a place to wallow and, in effect, hole up. Shaped like washbasins, gator holes may be twelve feet deep and many yards wide.

Although the resident alligator keeps the water clear of excessive vegetation, plants root and grow in the muddy soil thrown around the rim. Eventually, small trees arise, in which wading birds often nest. Bird droppings fertilize the soil below and encourage more growth. Meanwhile, fish wash into the hole and turtles enter, providing food for the gator. During droughts, the holes may be the only water source around for mammals and birds. Otters and raccoons come to drink. Gar and catfish lie close to the bottom ooze. Leopard frogs and pig frogs hide in the syrupy, green slime at water's edge. The frogs, fish, and turtles that escape the alligator survive to repopulate the surrounding wetlands when the rains return. Even more importantly, the water of the gator hole is a refuge for diatoms, protozoans, and minute crustaceans that are the first link in the wetlands food chain.

The evolutionary closeness between avian archosaurs, birds, and crocodilians like alligators is evinced by the fact that few other reptiles vocalize. The alligator does so in spades. There are two sounds made by animals that when I first heard them in the night truly elevated my hackles and made me feel as vulnerable as an australopithecine alone on the savanna. One was the thunder of lions on the African plains. The other was the mating bellow of a bull gator in the depths of the Okefenokee. Imagine it. In the blackness, the gator fills its lungs with air, puffing the sides of its blue-black body. Ripples fan out as the creature lifts its head and expels a blast of air from its lungs, which vibrate vocal folds in its neck expanding and contracting the skin over its throat. A deep, grumbling roar echoes through the swamp, followed by another and another, each seemingly louder than the one before. No other crocodilian makes such a thunderous vocal statement.

Alligator is an English corruption of the name the first Europeans to explore the Southeast gave to the big, toothy monster they saw prowling swamps and marshes: *el lagarto,* Spanish for "the lizard." At the time, alligators were the most numerous large animal in many parts of their range, which stretched from the Dismal Swamp on the border of North Carolina and Virginia to Texas. Today, they have reclaimed habitat in most of their original range. The states in which they live are North Carolina, South Carolina, Georgia, Florida, Alabama, Mississippi, Louisiana, Arkansas, Texas, and a very small area of southeastern Oklahoma.

When he traveled through Florida from 1774 to 1776, the naturalist William Bartram was amazed by the proliferation of alligators there. They were so numerous in the St. Johns River, he wrote in one of his journals, "that it would have been easy to have walked across on their heads."

Within a few decades of Bartram's observation, the alligator, like so many other wild animals, took on an economic significance. People discovered that its hide made beautiful leather, at first for saddlebags, then for products from purses to shoes. Hide hunting gained momentum throughout the nineteenth century. Year after year, the slaughter continued and alligators began to disappear from places in which they had abounded. Meanwhile, human activities destroyed alligator habitat. As a result of supply and demand, hides became more valuable. By 1969, the price was more than eight dollars a foot, in that era's money. As new laws restricted hunting, gator poachers, swamp-savvy and canny, prospered. Many traders of hides turned smuggler. Many times, with wildlife agents, I saw the seized hides of alligators, neatly bundled, some sporting feet and claws. The illegal trade prompted bans even on the sale of finished alligator products, spearheaded by New York City, a center of the trade.

Protection worked better than anyone expected, and alligators explosively procreated themselves back into abundance. States reopened tightly regulated hunting seasons, and alligator farms turned out hides from pen-raised gators. The problem of how to save the alligator was solved. The next problem was how to keep people safe from alligators.

Just as it is with cougars and coyotes, the rate of attacks on humans by alligators is going up. In 2005, Ricky L. Langley, a physician with the North Carolina Department of Health and Human Services, produced a research paper, "Alligator Attacks on Humans in the United States." He made no bones about it. "Encounters with alligators are increasing in the United States," he declared in the first sentence of his paper, going on to say that "as human population encroaches on the habitat of alligators, attacks and nuisance complaints increase."

Langley queried wildlife agencies in alligator-range states, but focused on Florida, which has the best records on alligator attacks. As noted above, that state has been keeping a tally on attacks since 1948. Georgia's Wildlife Resources Division, in comparison, began keeping records of attacks in 1980. Langley stated that from 1948 to 2004, "376 injuries and 15 deaths have been reported in the United States as a result of encounter with alligators." The total changed rapidly, lending credence to Langley's warning about the increasing frequency of attacks. Within eight years, the number of people killed by alligators had jumped by almost half that since record keeping began.

Three of those deaths, all women, occurred within a single week during May of 2006. First to die was a twenty-eight-year-old jogger out for an evening run through an area of Broward County where housing developments have replaced Everglades alligator habitat. Authorities theorized she might have been dragged into the water when she stopped to cool her feet in a canal, where an alligator, almost ten feet long, was later killed and found to have her arms in its stomach. Four days later, the partly eaten body of a forty-three-year-old woman was discovered in a canal near St. Petersburg. Her arm and hand were later recovered from the insides of an eight-and-a-half-foot alligator. The same day as her body was found, a twenty-three-year-old, snorkeling in the Ocala National Forest in Marion County, was attacked by an eleven-footer. Her husband and a friend spotted the animal with the woman in its jaws. They battled the gator over her body, which they managed to extract, but the victim was already dead from wounds to body and head and apparent drowning.

Another spate of attacks occurred during July 2012, when two teenagers were injured during one week in different parts of Florida. One of the attacks illustrates how alligators often venture into saline estuaries, where they prey on animals such as crabs and, at least on this occasion, people.

A fifteen-year-old boy was spearfishing in only three feet of water in a brackish creek at Keaton Beach, in the Big Bend area of North Florida, when a ten-foot alligator grabbed him across the chest. Thinking it was a shark, he screamed for his grandfather, who was nearby in a boat, and started struggling in an effort to escape the gator's grip. The boy's fight paid off and the alligator let go. Later, the youth and his grandfather returned to the creek, saw a gator in the same area, and shot it to death.

The other teen attack victim was swimming with friends in the Caloosahatchee River in Moore Haven, on the southwest shore of Lake Okeechobee. The seventeen-year-old lost his arm below the elbow during a valiant battle with an alligator that saw him survive the feared death roll. Twice. The alligator struck the teen seconds after one of his friends saw the creature and shouted a warning. The victim credited his ability to fight back to what he had learned from television shows—apparently the accurate kind—about alligators. Anticipating the roll, he locked his legs around the alligator's body, according to news reports of the incident. As the alligator rolled a second time, he managed to break loose, leaving his arm with the reptile. He screamed to his friends to get help as he made it to shore, where he stumbled and then fell to the ground. The youth told reporters that he fought to keep calm rather than hyperventilate, and used spider webs he found on the ground to stop the bleeding. His arm was found inside the alligator, an eleven-footer, when it was tracked down and killed by authorities.

A few months later, in September, near Orlando, an eighty-four-year-old woman lost her arm when an alligator dragged her into a canal that ran immediately next to residences in a mobile home park. A neighbor, who was sitting in his home having coffee, saw her foundering in the four-foot-deep water. He jumped in and pulled her out, only then seeing she was missing an arm below the shoulder. As he held her in his arms waiting for help to arrive, she mumbled "Gator," according to a media account. The woman, described as petite, was a widow who had moved to Florida from Maine after the death of her husband. When rescued, the woman was wearing just a slip. The rest of her clothes were discovered on a nearby dock, leading to speculation that she might have been disoriented and gone for a swim. The canal is linked to a lake with a large population of alligators and not regularly used for swimming.

Another attack on an elderly woman, eighty-three, resulted in one of the few fatalities caused by alligators outside Florida. Her body was discovered floating in the water of a lagoon at a high-end gated community called the Landings, near Savannah, Georgia, in October 2007. Her left arm, right hand, and a foot were missing. The body parts were later found in the stomach of an eight-foot alligator killed by a licensed alligator trapper. Officials speculated she was walking near the water when attacked. A Canadian, the woman was visiting the area, house-sitting for her son, and unfamiliar with alligators.

A bizarre death by alligator occurred in 2007 when a fugitive from the law's long arm ended up as gator bait. Surprised by police while breaking into a car in the parking lot of a Miami-Dade County convention center, he jumped into a pond, started screaming, and disappeared. His body was later found covered by alligators. In his haste, he apparently missed a sign by the pond warning that alligators prowled its waters. Jail would have been a better fate.

Golfers and alligators are a poor mix, given that attacks often occur around ponds and other water hazards on the links. Almost 10 percent of the alligator attacks analyzed in the Langley study occurred while the victim was retrieving a golf ball from water. It happened to a seventy-five-year-old man who went to pick up a ball from the edge of an irrigation pond. As he turned to rejoin his friends, an alligator lunged from the water, grabbed the golfer behind the knee, and threw him to the ground. There, the gator clamped its jaws on the man's shoulder as fellow golfers tried to pull him out of the animal's grasp. A frantic tug-of-war ensued as the alligator dragged its prey halfway into the water, then, lucky for the man, let go. Trappers later killed two alligators in the pond, one nine feet, the other six feet. The contents of the larger alligator's stomach indicated that someone had been feeding it. The golfer was severely slashed and bitten to the bone but recovered.

The damage that the crushing jaws of an alligator can cause may be much more than at first meets the eye, warns Langley in his study, noting that "massive internal injuries may occur." Beyond trauma lurks even more insidious danger. Many types of bacteria and other microbes, some of which can cause serious infections, have been cultured from the mouths of alligators, making treatments with antibiotics and other medications necessary, along with surgery.

Statistics from Langley's study show that the limbs are by far the parts of the body most often injured by alligator attacks. More males than females are victims. Of the 376 nonfatal cases studied, males were targets in 257, perhaps because more men than women engage in outdoor activities that bring them within range of gators, at least historically. Langley analyzed what victims were doing when attacked and found that the outdoor recreation topping the list—no surprise—was swimming, at 16.7 percent. Fishing (9.9 percent) was next, followed by retrieving golf balls (9.5 percent), wading (5.3 percent), and snorkeling (4.3 percent). Recreating aside, stupidity on the part of the victims can be blamed for the most attacks. More than 17 percent of the victims were messing around with the alligator that bit them, trying to catch or otherwise handle it. At the bottom of the list were gardening at water's edge, being on the bank for whatever reason, working on or falling out of a boat, walking near the water, and waterskiing or canoeing.

Langley's figures on the timing of nonfatal attacks is especially interesting, challenging conventional wisdom that the hours of darkness are most dangerous, because that is when alligators are most active. Ninety-seven of the attacks occurred between 6:00 P.M. and 6:00 A.M., while 172 took place between 6:00 A.M. and 6:00 P.M.

It stands to reason that small alligators usually bite humans out of fear, not hunger or aggression. Indeed, Langley's research indicates that if an alligator is less than eight feet long it will probably bite only once. That fits the scenario of a defensive bite and retreat from perceived danger. Even a pint-size gator, however, can deliver a painful wound. When large alligators attack, on the other hand, they usually mean business, biting repeatedly. Fully a third of the attacks studied by Langley involved more than one bite, and instead were fully mounted attacks often ending in serious injury or death. Such attacks, he suggests, may be attributed to predatory feeding behavior.

Over the years, apologists for alligators have claimed that serious attacks often come from females defending young, or individuals of either sex defending territory. Not so, says the Internet Center for Wildlife Damage Management (ICWDM. org), a nonprofit site that provides advice on animal threats, developed from solid scientific research. Based at the University of Nebraska, it is associated with researchers at several other prestigious universities as well. "Contrary to popular belief," states its document on alligators, "few attacks can be attributed to wounded or territorial alligators or females defending their nests or young."

More often than not, when the bodies of alligators that have attacked people are necropsied, they turn out to be physically sound, not undernourished or sick. A territorial defense by an alligator usually involves considerable sound and fury, more bluster than battery. An alligator hoping to deter an interloper will mount a highly conspicuous display atop the water, complete with hissing and snorts. When hunting prey, on the other hand, alligators engage in sneak attacks, staying out of sight until they launch an overwhelming assault. The teenager who lost his arm to an alligator in Moore Haven was unaware of its presence until his friends sounded the alarm. Almost all victims of attacks were similarly oblivious to the threat until it materialized.

In the southern portions of their range, such as South Florida, alligators may be active year-round. Mostly, alligators handle cold weather by lapsing into a state of dormancy, during which their metabolic processes slow. They may remain under water or lie on the bottom for long periods of time or den up in a burrow.

Even if territoriality is not a motivating factor in most attacks, their increased activity when alligators emerge from dormancy increases the chances of human encounters. Activity mounts during the spring seasons of courtship and mating, when alligators, their sex hormones churning, move about and are more agitated than at any other time of year. Even smaller, nonbreeding gators are caught up in the excitement, as many of them are displaced by the movement of their larger relatives. Perhaps it was not coincidence that the deaths of three Floridian women attacked by alligators in one week occurred in May, the height of the breeding season.

While the possibility that predator attacks by a large, hungry alligator are a fact of life anywhere alligators and people exist together, bites from chance encounters are more routine. And incidents in which alligators become a nuisance are commonplace. Most complaints about alligators—as opposed to violent episodes—emanate from places such as backyard ponds, canals, ditches, and streams, according to the Florida Fish and Wildlife Conservation Commission. The agency notes that other likely situations in which conflicts may develop are "when alligators wander into garages, swimming pools and golf course ponds." People also frequently encounter alligators when the animals leave the water to bask in the sun or are moving between wetlands.

Safety Tips: Alligators

If you live in alligator country, be aware that spring can be a risky time. Year round, there are commonsense precautions you can take to keep you safe. Here are some adapted from those suggested by the Florida Fish and Wildlife Conservation Commission:

Never handle, tease, or feed alligators. Give them plenty of space. Be especially wary when working or recreating around water, which seems obvious but bears repeating. Pay attention to warning signs and heed the advice they give. Keep pet dogs and cats out of the water. Especially, do not swim with your dog. An alligator that intends to sample your dog may change its mind and try a bigger piece of the pie. When fishing or camping around alligators, dispose of fish scraps and other items that alligators may consume. If you are bitten, even slightly, seek immediate medical attention to ward off infection.

CHAPTER 8

ALIEN INVASION:
Will Global Warming Trigger a Plague of Serpents?

Florida has other huge reptiles besides alligators to worry about. Giant exotic snakes are contesting the alligator's throne atop the food chain. As if alligators were not enough, Floridians now must contend with giant snakes in their midst, almost as if they lived in a real-life *Jurassic Park*.

A preview of what may lie in store for the Sunshine State occurred during the night of August 5, 2013, far to the north in Campbellton, a small city in Canada's province of New Brunswick. As two little boys slept peacefully in a second-floor apartment, death lurked in the ceiling above them. An African rock python, fourteen feet long and weighing one hundred pounds, had escaped from a glass enclosure that abutted the ceiling in another room and made its way through a small hole into the apartment's ventilation system. Creeping along pipes, the snake reached a point above the boys, where its weight collapsed the ceiling and sent the reptile tumbling into their room. The lifeless bodies of six-year-old Connor Barthe and his four-year-old brother Noah were discovered the next morning. An autopsy indicated that they had been asphyxiated, obviously by constriction in the powerful coils of the snake. The owner of the snake, as well as the apartment in which the boys slept and the pet shop below it, was a close friend of the boys' family. His young son, sleeping in another room, was unharmed.

The deaths of the two boys sent shock waves far beyond

Campbellton and sparked an outcry against the keeping of dangerous exotic pets in the province, which already had regulations in place prohibiting private ownership of the species of snake that killed the boys. Some experts said the deaths were the result of a tragic accident, when a panicked snake became entangled with the youngsters, but others speculated that the python was hungry and out to eat them. The African rock python, which reaches twenty feet in length, regularly preys on animals as large as warthogs and antelope in the wild. It is known as perhaps the most savage of the twenty-six species of pythons, nonvenomous constrictors that inhabit Africa, Asia, and Australia. It has attacked and killed humans in the wild.

The tragedy in Canada should send shivers down the spine of Floridians, because African rock pythons are on the loose in their state. In an online news piece *National Geographic* described the situation as a "Python 'Nightmare,'" as the African rock python joins the thousands—perhaps more than one hundred thousand—invasive Burmese pythons that already roam South Florida (September 14, 2009). Florida's thriving python population originates from a reservoir of escaped and released pets. Authorities often describe the Burmese python as rather docile, not threatening to people, which is why it has been favored by the pet trade. Tell that to the relatives of a two-year-old Florida girl who was killed by a pet Burmese python in 2009. Burmese pythons do behave rather calmly, while rock pythons are observably nasty and highly aggressive. In 2002, near Durban, South Africa, a twenty-foot rock python killed and swallowed a ten-year-old boy as his terrified friends watched. A handful of rock pythons have been found in Florida, including a few young and a female gravid with eggs, indicating "evidence of reproduction," according to the University of Florida Museum of Natural History website. Given that the two species have interbred in captivity, the prospect of the same mixing in the wild now looms. The news media are already talking about the hybrid "supersnake" that prowls Florida's backwaters. SyFy Channel, where are you?

The supersnake and its progenitors may threaten much more of the United States than Florida, according to maps released in 2008 by the U.S. Geological Survey. What is Florida's problem today could extend far beyond its borders tomorrow if the climate warms, as scientists predict. "Burmese pythons could find comfortable climatic conditions in roughly a third of the United States according to new climate maps developed by the U.S. Geological Survey (USGS)," an agency press release announced, sparking a rash of newspaper headlines warning of a python Armageddon. Under existing climatic conditions, according to the study, the snakes could make themselves at home as far north as Northern California and the Delmarva Peninsula, and all across the country's southern tier. By 2010, the potential range of the python shown on the maps edges into the lower Midwest and reaches Long Island, New York. One can imagine the havoc pythons might cause among the row houses of Nassau County and Archie Bunker's Queens.

The USGS announcement contained an especially important sentence. Here it is, the emphasis being mine: "Although other factors such as type of food available and suitable shelter also play a role, Burmese pythons *and other giant constrictor snakes* have shown themselves to be highly adaptable to new environments." Read the words in italics here as "rock pythons and anacondas." The green anaconda, a giant boa from the South American tropics, may have a foothold in South Florida. Several have been sighted in the state, and a twelve-footer was captured at a fish camp in Osceola County in January 2010. A few common boa constrictors are breeding on one estate near Miami, but their numbers and expansion have been controlled. Other giant snakes seen in Florida, and perhaps waiting in the wings to reproduce, include the yellow anaconda and reticulated python.

The snake at the core of the scare, the Burmese python, is prized as a pet not only for its alleged docility but because of its attractive color pattern of brown blotches bordered with black—some are albino—and its availability. It can be bought at bargain prices for an exotic snake, at $80 or less retail and $20 at pet shows. Figures from the U.S. Fish and Wildlife Service show that approximately ninety-nine thousand Burmese pythons were imported to the United States between 1996 and 2006, a fivefold increase from the previous two decades.

Commerce has drained native wild populations even though thousands of pythons have been bred in captivity. The species is classified by the World Conservation Union as "near threatened" in the wild due to capture for the pet trade and hunting for skins. Ironically, there are probably more Burmese pythons slithering around Florida than in their natural range, which covers much of Southeast Asia. Beyond the limits of its main range, isolated populations are pocketed in India and even in Sichuan, China.

Typical of boas and pythons, the Burmese species usually seizes prey in its needle-sharp recurved teeth, then quickly and repeatedly loops its sinuous body around the prey. If it can anchor its tail to a nearby object or the limb of the prey for leverage and stability, so much the better. To the untrained eye, it may appear as if constriction goes on unabated until the victim is crushed. Both assumptions are incorrect. The snake squeezes its coils in pulses, to conserve muscular energy and as a tactic. Each time the victim exhales, the coils tighten their grip and the chest cavity of the victim collapses inward, unable to expand, until suffocation, not crushing, ends in death.

I have handled boa constructors, anacondas, and pythons up to a dozen feet or so in length. The power even one coil can exert upon one's arm is impressive, and frightening, especially in the case of the larger species. A boa constrictor has sinuous strength, to be sure, but an anaconda feels as if it were made of pliable steel.

A huge snake, the Burmese python can surpass twenty feet in length and weigh more than two hundred pounds. They grow so fast that a hatchling twenty inches long might reach eight feet in a year. One of the reasons why pet owners release pythons is that the little hatchling that is easy to handle swiftly becomes a monster stronger than its owner. Burmese pythons are strong and big enough to kill and eat animals as large as white-tailed deer and adult American alligators, which are as big as or bigger than an adult human. Generally, a Burmese python will feed indiscriminately on almost any mammal or bird it can catch, as well as reptiles, amphibians, and fish.

The voracity of the Burmese python has been verified by a USGS 2011 study that paints it as the grim reaper of native wildlife. University of Florida researchers who analyzed the odoriferous contents of Burmese python digestive tracts found the remains of fourteen species of mammals, five species of birds, and one species of reptile. This alien invader is eating its way through Florida's indigenous wildlife, sucking up animals, from woodrats to Florida panthers, like a living vacuum cleaner. Published in the *Proceedings of the National Academy of Sciences* by Michael E. Dorcas of Davidson College and an army of colleagues, the study links the Burmese python to what the USGS referred to as "precipitous declines in formerly common mammals in Everglades National Park." According to the U.S. Geolgical Survey press release announcing the findings, "The study, the first to document the ecological impacts of this invasive species, strongly supports that animal communities in this 1.5-million-acre park have been markedly altered by the introduction of pythons within 11 years of their establishment as an invasive species. Mid-sized mammals are the most dramatically affected."

"Pythons are wreaking havoc on one of America's most beautiful, treasured and naturally bountiful ecosystems," noted U.S. Geological Survey director Marcia McNutt, quoted in an agency release dated January 30, 2012.

A hint of the invasion of serpents to come occurred when a Burmese python was seen in the Everglades in 1979. Not until the middle of the 1990s was another found, but after that, sightings progressed geometrically. Scientific curiosity turned to crisis mode in 2003 when biologists confirmed that pythons were indeed breeding in the Everglades. Since then, the snakes have extended their holdings. Healthy python populations have been observed in Big Cypress National Preserve north of the glades, in state parks, within cities and suburbs, and in water-management areas.

Their rampant multiplication has been facilitated by the way Burmese pythons reproduce in assembly-line fashion, as many as a hundred eggs in one clutch. The hatchlings have an immediate edge, because they are larger than hatchlings of native species and thus less susceptible to smaller predators. They are, however, vulnerable at this stage to black bears, panthers, alligators, and large birds of prey, but quickly become too big for even the top predators to handle. With few, if any, competitors or predators as adults, however, Burmese pythons have free rein of the land they have infiltrated. Like coyotes, Burmese pythons can subsist on a highly diverse diet and in many different habitats. These multiple advantages may allow pythons to compete with native snakes and other predators for food, habitat, and space. Thus, native species suffer. The pythons also are noted for long-distance travel.

A female python studied by University of Florida scientists traveled more than 35 miles from its capture site during the course of a summer.

Given all its ponds, lakes, wetlands, and canals, Florida is tailor-made for Burmese pythons, which are semiaquatic, extremely fond of habitat around water. They are superb swimmers that travel long distances by water and, like alligators, have made use of Florida's canal network to expand their territory. Canals also afford them access to housing developments and other areas with large concentrations of humans. They have crossed the six miles of Florida Bay separating Key Largo from the mainland and could easily navigate farther on through the Keys. Isolated on their islands, wildlife on the Keys would be at the mercy of the pythons. The snakes already have preyed on the imperiled Key Largo woodrat. Burmese pythons regularly prowl wading bird rookeries and climb trees with ease, putting nestlings as well as adults at risk. Biologists worry they could decimate not only common wading birds but rare species, such as the limpkin and white ibis.

Everglades mammals seem to be suffering most from python depredations. In the southern reaches of the park, where pythons took hold early, there has been "a nearly complete disappearance of raccoons, rabbits and opossums," according to the USGS. The raccoon population dropped 99.3 percent, opossums 98.9 percent, and once-common marsh rabbits and cottontails were not observed at all. Raccoons and opossums, especially, often forage at water's edge, increasing the odds that while looking for a meal, they become one. Bobcats, down 87.5 percent, are also disappearing down the maws of the pythons. If one disbelieves that a python can prey upon bobcats, known for their own brand of ferocity, consider this: Burmese pythons sometimes feed on leopards in their native habitat. Fears are that the python could endanger the few Florida panthers remaining in the wild, probably less than two hundred in all.

The USGS researchers compared results inside the park with surveys of ecologically similar areas north of it not yet invaded by pythons. In those areas, mammal numbers were similar to those in the park before pythons proliferated. The scientists who authored the paper noted that the timing and geographic patterns of the mammal declines they documented matched up well with the timing and geographic spread of pythons. Moreover, decline began very soon after the advance wave of snakes swept over an area. Verification of the study's results was available, although in a rather messy form. The same mammals that were disappearing regularly turned up in the digestive tracts of pythons that had been removed from the park and killed.

Scientists who did the research suggested that one reason the region has been swept clean of native mammals in such a short time is that these animals are what the researchers called "naive" about large snakes. No snakes the size of Burmese pythons have inhabited the eastern United States for millions of years. The defense mechanisms of native mammals, therefore, have not adapted to dealing with them. The impact of the python on mammals may go beyond the species that were surveyed by scientists. "It is possible that other mammal species, including at-risk ones, have declined as well because of python predation, but at this time, the status of those species is unknown," Robert Reed, a USGS scientist and coauthor of the Everglades study, commented in the USGS press release. The disappearance of so many different mammals is bound to throw the entire Everglades ecosystem out of whack and profoundly impact natural communities well beyond the sloughs and sawgrass wilderness of the park.

"Wildlife managers are concerned that these snakes,

which can grow to over 20 feet long and more than 250 pounds, pose a danger to state- and federally listed threatened and endangered species as well as to humans," said Reed, who was also involved in the study that predicted pythons could extend their range beyond Florida. "Several endangered species," he noted, have already been found in the digestive systems of the snakes. "Pythons could have even more significant environmental and economic consequences if they were to spread from Florida to other states," he warned.

The study of python impact on mammals in Everglades National Park was exceedingly thorough. Systematically working roads within the park by night, the researchers followed the same routes taken for a survey in 1996 and 1997, before pythons were established, so that they could compare results. From 2003 to 2011 they logged thirty-nine thousand miles, counting live animals as well as roadkill. The scope of the decline shocked them.

"The magnitude of these declines underscores the apparent incredible density of pythons in Everglades National Park and justifies the argument for more intensive investigation into their ecological effects, as well as the development of effective control methods," said Dorcas, lead author of the study, a professor at Davidson College in North Carolina and author of the book *Invasive Pythons in the United States.* "Such severe declines in easily seen mammals bode poorly for the many species of conservation concern that are more difficult to sample but that may also be vulnerable to python predation."

A document from the University of Florida on pythons and the problems they cause noted that the impact of the snakes on endangered species could be serious. The document also raised an issue seldom spoken about by officialdom but always lurking in the background: "Human safety is also a concern. There is no evidence that wild Burmese pythons hunt humans; however, on several occasions large captive Burmese pythons have killed their owners."

Indeed they have. In 1996, a nineteen-year-old man was found dead on the bloody floor of a hallway in his Bronx, New York, apartment building. His thirteen-foot Burmese python was coiled around him. In 2002, a forty-three-year-old Aurora, Colorado, man was strangled to death by his ten-foot-long Burmese python, which had wrapped itself around his neck. It took seven firefighters and two police officers to uncoil the snake from the man's body, according to news reports. A forty-eight-year-old Ohio man suffered a similar fate in 2006 when doctors could not save him after he was found with his pet python necklace. The python that killed the two-year-old in Florida escaped from its cage before it attacked her. It belonged to her mother's boyfriend. They were convicted of third-degree murder, manslaughter, and child neglect and were each sentenced to twelve years in prison. An appellate court later upheld the main charge of manslaughter and the twelve-year prison sentence for both.

If pet Burmese pythons, used to being handled, kill people, why not wild ones? The stage is set for a python to grab a toddler that happens to momentarily stray out of sight while playing in the backyard; for a hiker to stumble into a python in the brush and end up encoiled; or for someone sleeping it off on a park bench to become python bait. For all the claims about their docility, the human fatalities racked up by pet Burmese pythons show that they can and will kill people.

A battle to the death between man and python occurred in May 2013, when a twenty-three-year-old marine biology student, Jason Leon, knifed to death a huge Burmese python after he and the huge reptile tangled with one another. At eighteen feet, eight inches long, it turned out to be the largest of the species killed in Florida to that date. The snake apparently had not eaten for a long time; its digestive tract contained only a single bird feather.

Leon and his friends spotted the snake in the brush near Florida City. Leon, who had experience keeping pet snakes, grabbed the python behind the head to pull it out of the vegetation for a better look. The snake came out, all right—and just kept coming. Leon was unaware of its size until it emerged from the vegetation and started looping coils around his leg. He and two friends held off the serpent until a friend handed him a knife and he decapitated it. Newspapers reported that the snake weighed only 128 pounds, some 200 pounds below normal weight for a python of that length. I cannot help but wonder if the snake's starved condition made a difference in the battle.

Burmese pythons are taking a cue from alligators throughout South Florida, slithering out of their hidden havens in the marshes and swamps into places where they are most unwelcome. Here is just a small sampling of reported encounters with people:

On Christmas Day, 2011, members of the Miami-Dade Fire Rescue Venom Response unit removed a thirteen-foot python from a backyard swimming pool in Miami.

The same unit responded in August 2013 when a python, another thirteen-footer, surprised a Hialeah homeowner when he opened the door of his backyard shed.

In October 2008, a twelve-foot python caused alarm as it slithered around a shopping plaza in Jupiter Farms, Palm Bach County.

A large snake frightened a Vero Beach woman in July 2013. She feared it was a rattlesnake but it turned out to be an eight-foot Burmese python.

A farmer in Homestead called authorities when he saw a suspicious tail, scaly and wiggly, sticking out from under a feed container. It belonged to an eleven-foot python that had been eating his chickens and goats.

Golfers at a luxury club in St. Petersburg became understandably nervous in June 2013 when they saw a python at least a dozen feet long hanging around near the twelfth tee.

The Burmese pythons creeping into Florida's backyards are huge, dangerous beasts, and odds are that they will eventually follow the lead of their pet counterparts and kill someone, even if they are not the most aggressive of the big snakes in their behavior toward humans.

That distinction belongs to the "nightmare" African rock

python. Africa's largest snake, the rock python is somewhat smaller than its Burmese relative, generally maxing out at twenty feet. What it lacks in size, however, it makes up for in ferocity. Zookeepers know that rock pythons are much more inclined to bite than most of their kin. Although nonvenomous, python teeth can inflict a severe wound. Once embedded in the flesh, their recurved design makes removal a difficult and painful task.

Rock pythons inhabit most of sub-Saharan Africa except for deserts. Like the Burmese python, they are partly aquatic. The only African rock python I have seen in the wild was in water. Many years ago, I was on patrol with rangers in Kenya's Lake Nakuru National Park when one of my companions pointed toward a small stream that meandered through the grassland. Standing along the stream bank were about a dozen marabou storks. These ubiquitous birds have a range similar to that of the rock python. They are huge, standing up to five feet high, weighing up to twenty pounds (but usually half that), with wings that sometimes span more than ten feet. Armed with a long, massive bill, the storks are voracious scavengers and predators. Like pythons, they eat almost anything they can overcome and swallow; they regularly savage and eat the flamingoes that throng on East Africa's saline lakes.

The storks were watching something in the water. As we neared the stream, I saw the head of a big snake poking above a riffle. Behind it, visible in calm water, was about sixteen feet of body. It was a rock python, obviously considering whether or not it could pick off a stork.

Trouble was, the storks were eyeing the python back as a potential meal. One stork is no match for a python; a bunch of them, perhaps. We watched for the better part of an hour. Every so often, the snake would turn its head or adjust its body, its eyes on the storks all the while. Each time the python edged its body, the storks adjusted their positions. It was a classic standoff, and finally the snake slid away, heading downstream in search of easier pickings.

Rock pythons in Florida have been found largely around water. Typical places include small canals, housing developments, agricultural areas, and seasonally flooded wetlands like those of the Everglades. Mostly, the pythons have been seen around the glades and in the Miami area. In January 2011, one was captured by wildlife authorities far to the north, in the city of Tarpon Springs on the state's west coast. A man walking his dog near an apartment complex came upon the snake sunning itself next to the Anclote River. When measured, it was more than fourteen feet long.

Kenneth Krysko, a herpetologist at the Florida Museum of Natural History, described the rock python in an online *National Geographic* news story as "so mean they come out of the egg striking . . . This is just one vicious animal," and a danger to "almost any warm-blooded animal that is big enough to ingest" (September 14, 2009). Big enough? A child, certainly. An adult, possibly. If rock pythons proliferate, Floridians may look upon the Burmese python invasion as the good old days. A hint of things to come: in September 2013, a ten-foot rock python killed a ninety-pound husky outside its owner's home near Miami.

As far as the future is concerned, whether pythons will spread beyond Florida is an open question. Of the two species, Burmese and African rock python, the latter has the least chance of moving from Florida's subtropical warmth to temperate climates in the north. Rock pythons do range into areas of South Africa where the climate verges on temperate, but in general need tropical and subtropical climate. Whether future generations of rock pythons could adapt to slightly cooler temperatures in the event the species edges northward is uncertain but possible. Michael Dorcas raised this point in a study on captive Burmese pythons published in 2011, conducted at the Savannah River Ecology Laboratory of the Savannah River nuclear site in South Carolina. The study was aimed at testing whether the pythons could survive the cooler environment of South Carolina.

As an aside, years ago I was given a rat snake while visiting the Savannah River laboratory. I took it home in a sack, which I held on my lap during the flight home. As we were under way, I became involved in my own version of *Snakes on a Plane.* As a flight attendant handed me coffee, the sack began to move, whereupon she demanded to know what it held. "A rat snake," I said. Moments later, passengers verged on panic. I could hear the whisper spreading through the aircraft that I had a "rattlesnake" aboard. When I debarked from the plane, the pilot and the rest of the crew glared at me with unconcealed fury.

In the study at Savannah River, Dorcas and his colleagues released ten wild-caught male Burmese pythons from Florida into an enclosure, which was designed for the experiment and open to the elements so the snakes would be exposed to weather typical of the region. The snakes prospered at first. With the onset of fall and cooler temperatures, they basked more in the sun and began to take refuge in underground sheltering areas that were part of the enclosure's design. They survived even temperatures in the low forties. As temperatures dropped toward the freezing mark, the snakes began to die. The likely cause of death, in biology tech speak, was "inappropriate thermoregulatory behavior." In layman's language, the snakes did not take advantage of the underground refuges provided for them. Two snakes did seek cover underground but they, too, perished during a highly unusual cold snap during early January.

The cold snap, which lasted ten days, sent temperatures into the thirties in the Everglades, killed at least three rock pythons and thousands of Burmese pythons. Some biologists said the die-off signaled that climate would limit or even eliminate the invader. On the other side of the coin, when the temperatures returned to normal, immense numbers of pythons still inhabited Florida. It is a case of a glass half empty or half full. You could say that perhaps half the pythons in Florida died. But there is no escaping that both species of pythons took on the worst winter weather Florida could throw at them—and survived.

Despite the fact that none of the snakes in the experiment at the Savannah River laboratory survived, the study, published in the journal *Biological Invasions,* suggested that Burmese pythons could extend their range northward for a number of reasons. As the snakes edge north, each succeeding generation would become more acclimated to cooler temperatures. Adaptation might be behavioral as well as physiological. Natural selection might weed out individuals that did not display "appropriate thermoregulatory behavior," said the researchers. In other words, they might learn to get under cover when the temperatures drop. Nature, moreover, could very well provide deep cover farther underground, and this with more stable temperature than the refuges in the experimental enclosure.

Another factor that comes into play is that not all Burmese pythons come from hot climates. A 2008 paper in the *Bulletin of the Chicago Herpetological Society* analyzed the distribution of the Burmese python in its native Asia. Evidence indicates that the snakes live in parts of Nepal and Bhutan that fringe on the foothills of the Himalayas, where the climate is not exactly stifling. An isolated population, which may or may not have been introduced, lives far to the north in China's Sichuan Province.

The range lends credence to a statement in the Dorcas study: "Burmese pythons originating from more temperate localities within their native range may be more tolerant of cold temperatures and would presumably be more likely to successfully become established in temperate areas of North America."

Scientists, including those of the USGS, are focusing continued research on trying to figure out where the pythons and even other giant snakes—anacondas come to mind—will go next. Outside of the nation's northern tier, it could be anywhere.

Safety Tips: Pythons

The rules for keeping safe from pythons are not much different than those that apply to other wild creatures that one might encounter in the field or at the doorstep. Leave them alone.

Other than that, use common sense. If there is even a small chance of pythons in the area, keep very close tabs on children. Keep landscape near the home or play area free of brush or, in the case of snakes, debris under which they can hide. Keep lids on containers for trash and other items, not to keep pythons from feeding on garbage—they do not—but to prevent them from holing up inside the barrel or dumpster. There is an old saying that a snake can crawl through any opening big enough for its nose to enter. Make sure your residence has no openings for snakes to enter. The last-mentioned precaution makes sense in python country not just because of the constrictors. It works for venomous snakes as well. And some of the most toxic and dangerous of all live in the same countryside as Florida's pythons.

CHAPTER 9

PROWLING POISONERS:
The Venomous Snakes Next Door

D r. James A. Oliver, a leading herpetologist of his day, was the only person ever to head the American Museum of Natural History and the Bronx Zoo and the New York Aquarium of the New York Zoological Society. At one time or another, I as well worked for all three, although under Oliver only at the museum. Over the years until he passed away in 1981, he became a good friend and a very important mentor, teaching me not only about reptiles and amphibians but about the whole natural world and its conservation. He was a scientist to the core but lived far from the ivory tower, forging a reputation as a talented popular writer, a bon vivant, and a splendid raconteur.

One of his tales involved an unlucky young man who appeared at his office when he was curator of reptiles at the Bronx Zoo, a post he held in his younger days, before he became a top administrator. One morning Oliver's secretary buzzed him to say that a disheveled and distraught young man was in the lobby of the zoo's neoclassical main building, where I later had my own office. He was pleading to see someone in the reptile department, the offices of which were just a few feet away from the reception desk. The secretary, upset herself, said that the visitor claimed to have been bitten by a snake.

Oliver went to the waiting room and found the man, who was sweating, his eyes bulging and darting about, and obviously in great pain.

"Oy uz itten eye ah cop'had," the man croaked, frantically pointing toward his mouth. Oliver asked him to speak
more slowly and distinctly. As Oliver told me, "He gesticulat-
ed frantically, pointing toward his mouth and trying to speak
clearly."

"Oy uz itten by ah thnake, a cop'had thnake," struggled
the man, desperation on his beet-red face. The last word,
said Oliver, was a "slowly hissed scream." With that the man
stuck out his tongue, which was bloated, blistered, and black-
ened. Oliver had plenty of experience with snakebites, but
never on someone's tongue. Astonished, he asked where the
incident with the snake had happened. "Ina ahr, in Phelphia
lash niht," the man replied.

Oliver called for medical help and the man was treated.
As it turned out, the man was a merchant seaman whose
ship had stopped at Philadelphia. Somehow, while on liberty,
he took an excursion into the nearby countryside, where he
had found a very small baby snake, which he managed to get
into a jar without being bitten. He returned to his vessel and
displayed the snake to his shipmates. When they all headed out on a pub crawl, he took the snake with him. As they
downed more than a few at a waterfront saloon, he dumped
the snake atop the bar. Frightened, it coiled and flicked out
its tongue. The seaman's buddies dared him to try and touch
the snake's tongue with his own. He took them up on it. Seeing the offending tongue presented by the sailor, the infant
snake did what any good serpent would do and struck.

If what happened is hard to believe, what transpired next
is even more so. Instead of calling for an ambulance or going to a hospital in Philadelphia, the snakebit man took the
advice of his fellow drunks and opted to seek help at a zoo.
Not the Philadelphia Zoo, which was easily reachable, but the
Bronx Zoo, almost ninety miles away. Somehow, he was able
to hop a train in Philadelphia, ride to Manhattan during the

night, and then, either by subway or taxi, take the long trip to the northern Bronx, where he finally received the help he needed.

Saloons are not normal habitat for copperheads, but in many cases, cities are. Copperheads have been found in Philadelphia, at least historically, according to the Pennsylvania Amphibian and Reptile Survey, which is developing a herpetological map of the state, in association with state and federal conservation and wildlife agencies. This species, whose bite is rarely lethal, is, by its quiet, unobtrusive behavior, able to survive in urban and suburban surroundings from which other venomous snakes have been eliminated. Indeed, there are records of copperheads in recent years from wooded pockets of New York City.

Copperheads are among the several species of venomous snakes that regularly turn up in gardens, backyards, and even inside buildings. The likelihood of suburban and urban dwellers encountering copperheads and serpents with a toxic bite is increasing in many areas, due to reasons somewhat different from those that are causing other dangerous wild creatures to come among us. Venomous serpents, unlike most of the other creatures described in this book, are not wide-ranging travelers, so the two-way traffic analogy does not explain their urban and suburban presence. Few animals have suffered such intense efforts at extirpation as venomous snakes; perhaps more than any other creatures, they are the victims of a shoot-on-sight mentality rooted in ancient human antipathy for snakes in general. Thus, venomous snakes have not proliferated in secret wilderness havens. Except in cases where floodwaters have routed them out of their holes or when there have been local reproductive bursts, they have seldom invaded human habitat in the way of coyotes or alligators. The traffic, if the analogy holds, is mostly one-way, with people moving into *their* habitat.

The *Los Angeles Times* put it well in a story on May 16, 2005: "With the region's development encroaching into the deserts, mountains and foothills, clashes between man and serpent show no sign of slowing." The *New York Times,* in 2006, noted that the expansion of Los Angeles and Orange Counties into the desert is putting more people than ever into the backyard of rattlesnakes. The reports on California could also describe boom cities throughout the Southwest and in the Southeast as well, although the terrain may differ.

Few animals—not even sharks—evoke such universal dread as venomous serpents. People otherwise acclimated to the natural world can react with unmitigated horror to the possibility of a poisonous snake lurking under a leaf pile. Although the fear is by no means universal, a goodly part of humanity fears serpents so innately, it seems almost part of our DNA. And this fear extends to all snakes, even though only a relative few possess what so many humans view as a literal kiss of death.

The number of people bitten annually by venomous snakes in the United States has remained relatively steady for years: about twelve thousand cases. Various agencies and organizations differ slightly on the average number of fatalities, with the federal Centers for Disease Control stating "about five" and the American Academy of Family Physicians putting the figure at no more than a dozen. That said, indications are mounting that some species of venomous snakes may be more actively moving around their present habitats and encountering more people than in the past. Meanwhile, suspicions have arisen among medical experts that the venom of some species is evolving more zing to the ounce, a rise in toxicity that enhances their lethality. Lurking in the background, too, is the possibility that the same warming climate that could send giant pythons slithering far north of Florida could change the range maps of some venomous species as well.

People concerned about snakebite should first know their enemy. Of the approximately three thousand species of living snakes, about two hundred are known to be venomous, including about a dozen and a half in the United States, with the exact number depending on which taxonomists one believes. These snakes fall into four groups of species and subspecies: the coral snake, the copperhead, the water moccasin, or cottonmouth, and the rattlesnake. There are a few so-called "rear-fanged" snakes on the southern border that are mildly venomous but seldom, if ever, considered a threat. Rattlesnake species number fifteen, and along with copperheads and cottonmouths, belong to a group called pit vipers, because of a pit-like structure between the nostrils and eye that is a heat sensor. It makes them living heat-seeking missiles, able to home in on the body heat of warm-blooded prey in the dead of night. According to the American Academy of Family Physicians, 99 percent of snakebites in the United States come from this group.

The other venomous serpent in the United States is the coral snake. Scientists classify it in a group called the elapids, which includes the cobras. Coral snakes are warm-weather creatures. The eastern species ranges from extreme southeastern North Carolina to southern Texas, for the most part hugging coastal areas. The Arizona coral snake inhabits south-central Arizona and a bit of southwestern New Mexico. They have extremely potent venom but, being secretive and unaggressive, are responsible for only a score or so bites each year.

Elapids and pit vipers produce venom in a pair of glands similar to salivary glands in humans and many other animals. Snake venom, in fact, is saliva modified by evolution to be a means of killing prey. Once introduced, venom not only immobilizes or kills but initiates the digestive process, breaking down flesh. Its use as a defensive weapon is a side benefit. In 1962, when conflict was heating up in the tropical jungles of Southeast Asia, the Department of the Navy issued a manual for Naval and Marine Corps personnel produced by a committee of top herpetologists. The manual contained a statistic dramatically demonstrating that defense is a secondary function of venom: no signs of envenomation develop in between 3 percent and 40 percent of bites by venomous species. Faced with the need to defend itself, the serpent may withhold venom for when it has to feed itself. Typically, an average of 20 percent of all strikes do not involve envenomation.

The toxicity of snake venom varies considerably between species. The fact that the seaman mentioned above was bitten on the tongue, of all places, and still remained on his feet testifies to the fact that copperhead venom is not particularly potent. Bear in mind that the amount of venom was probably small as well. Some rattlesnakes, on the other hand, are armed with venom thirty thousand times more toxic than strychnine.

The chemistry of venoms and their impact on the body of the victim is highly complex. Gone is the old scientific classification of venom into three categories according to physiological activity: neurotoxins that attack the nervous system, hemotoxins that attack the blood, and cardiotoxins that attack the heart and related organs. Research has revealed that venoms are a witch's brew of toxic ingredients, mostly proteins, which can attack multiple organ systems.

Even so, however, the venom of each group of serpents has its own trademark symptoms and overt damage. Elapid venom may damage blood cells and organs but is marked by the way its neurotoxins cause paralysis. Pit viper bites cause traumatic tissue damage around the location of the bite, inability of blood to coagulate, and damage to heart, lungs, kidneys, and blood vessels. Pain erupts almost as soon as a rattlesnake strikes. The site of the bite swells and skin and tissue around the bite deteriorates, while nausea and sweating occur.

Each of the two glands that make and store venom is sheathed with connective tissue that contracts when the snake's nervous system signals for venom discharge. The venom flows through ducts to the fangs, located in the fore of the upper jaw, which transmit venom to the victim. Together, fangs, ducts, and glands constitute the "venom apparatus." The fangs of elapids are relatively short and strike by biting, even chewing, with venom seeping down a groove in each of them. Even cobras must sometimes bite more than once to introduce enough venom. Coral snakes have such small teeth, they may not penetrate clothing and even skin, one of the reasons for their low threat level.

The design of pit viper fangs, on the other hand, is reptilian high-tech. These snakes were in possession of the hypodermic needle long before humans invented it. An inch long in some species, the fangs are hollow rather than grooved and inject venom rather than bite. When not in use, the fangs lie back in the jaw, out of the way. During a strike, as the jaws open to a tremendous gape, the fangs pivot up and forward so that they puncture the victim almost horizontally. The motion of the puncture is more a stabbing action, driven by powerful jaw muscles, than a bite.

Rattlesnakes are native to most states, but the section of the country that has a corner on them is the Southwest, from Texas to California. Texas has ten species, New Mexico seven, Arizona thirteen, and California and Nevada seven. The southern parts of the last-mentioned states have the most rattlesnake diversity. Rattlesnakes are abundant in many southeastern states but not as diverse. Florida, for example, has three species of rattlesnakes. One, a race of the timber rattlesnake, is found only in a few northern counties. Another, the pygmy rattlesnake, is between a foot and two feet long, with relatively mild venom. I once had one strike repeatedly at my boot without leaving a mark. These little snakes, while not to be disrespected, are remarkably docile and one of the few venomous species I have allowed myself to handle. During the summer of 1975, scores of pygmy rattlesnakes that turned up in a new suburb of Miami caused a major panic among homeowners, who went so far as to dig up their precious shrubbery to remove snake cover. Only one person was bitten, a sixteen-year-old boy, on the finger. His symptoms were mild. The remaining species of rattlesnake in Florida is the eastern diamondback, which ranges sandy coastal scrub from North Carolina to Louisiana. It is often found among palmettos. Adults usually grow to about six feet in length, but some reach eight feet and even larger. With one-inch fangs and extremely potent venom, it is one of the world's most dangerous snakes. The slightly smaller western diamondback, which ranges from Arkansas to southern California, is almost as menacing. The two diamondbacks strike and kill more Americans than any other venomous snakes.

Diamondbacks generally stay away from people, but where they are abundant they are not shy about approaching homes. In September 2010, a Georgia woman killed a seven-foot diamondback on the road just outside her home. In September 2009, an elderly couple in Manatee County, Florida, needed a trapper to remove a four-and-a-half-foot diamondback from their property. The same day, in the same county, a woman saw a six-foot diamondback slide into the shrubs near her front door. Her husband killed it to protect his family. He had good reason. In 2000, a two-year-old Manatee County boy died after a diamondback bit him as he played in his backyard.

Even more toxic than the diamondback is the Mojave rattlesnake, which ranges from West Texas to the western counties of Southern California. Seldom more than four feet long, it can be mistaken for a small western diamondback, because it too has diamond-like markings. The high toxicity of the Mojave rattler's venom was evident when one bit a six-year-old boy camping with his family in California in July 2012. The boy foamed at the mouth, vomited, and within a short time began to lose muscular control and have breathing difficulties. It took forty-two bottles of antivenom to stabilize him.

The rattlesnake with the highest potential for contact with people unfamiliar with venomous snakes is the timber rattlesnake, which has an original range stretching from East Texas and Kansas to the Atlantic Seaboard, south to the Gulf States, covering some of the most densely populated regions of the country. Had it not been extirpated from so much of its habitat, it would be involved in many more encounters. In much of the East, this five-foot snake is the only rattlesnake. Although it is on the endangered lists of many states and has been eliminated from most settled areas, pockets of these snakes persist amid humans. Some of them can be found in the suburbs of New York City and Washington, D.C.

In July 2011, police issued a warning to residents of Stony Point, New York, forty-four miles from Manhattan, after a fifty-four-year-old man was bitten by a timber rattlesnake on his property. The man reported seeing several of the snakes within a few days of being bitten. He was treated and released from a local hospital.

I had one experience with a timber rattler that was too close for comfort but proved that venomous snakes are not necessarily aggressive toward humans. From the time they were toddlers, my two daughters and my son have been exposed to snakes. Indeed, they grew up with snakes, because when I was a zoo curator and during the years I handled animals on television, I kept several snakes in my home. I had forgotten, however, that familiarity can breed complaisance, or a disregard for danger. One day I was out in my yard and my young son, then in elementary school, was sitting in my unpaved driveway. My home is surrounded by woods and swamp and well populated by wildlife. I noticed that he was playing with something on the ground. Instinct told me to take a look. There in front of him was a little snake, which even from a distance I could tell was not one of the charming ringnecked snakes that were always entering our home under the front door. My hackles went up and I told my son to stay still. Coming closer, I saw the beginning nub of a rattle, the so-called button on the snake's tail tip. Ever so gently, I gripped the creature behind the head and removed it, releasing into the back woods a baby timber rattlesnake.

About thirty miles distant from my home lies the town of Glastonbury, a major bedroom community of Connecticut's capital, Hartford. The eastern and southern parts of the town, and towns bordering it, contain one of the few thriving timber-rattlesnake populations in the state. The core of the population, probably the largest in the state, is based on a small mountain in a state forest. The snakes, however, regularly wander out of their population base, which has brought them into contact with people on a regular basis. That is, since 1990. Then, the town's population was less than eight thousand souls. It has since grown almost 300 percent, and many of the subdivisions have been built near and even in timber-rattlesnake homeland.

Even so, only a few people have been bitten, one of them a researcher who was handling snakes in the field. The most recent bite was in the neighboring town of Marlborough, in 2009. A forty-five-year-old man was at a backyard picnic when a rattler emerged from a leaf pile. He attempted to pick it up on a stick—bad move—and it bit him. He was treated at a hospital. He was lucky. Between May 2010 and April 2011, two men were killed at the western fringe of the rattler's range in the same Texas county, Bastrop, by timber rattlesnakes.

Reading the account, I was reminded of an incident I saw in which people through ignorance put themselves within reach of a timber rattlesnake. It was on the Blue Ridge Parkway in Shenandoah National Park, Virginia. A large timber rattler was on the roadside, recovering from what apparently was a glancing blow from a passing car. Several people had stopped to get a closer look. They crowded around it, presumably thinking it was too injured to move, which I knew was not the case. (Even a mortally injured snake can bite. A California man who ran over a rattler with his dirt bike was bitten by the head he had cut off to take home as a souvenir.) A few of the curious stood only a few feet away, well within the rattlesnake's reach. I alerted them to the danger, then left. Perhaps those gawkers were lucky; timber rattlers are not particularly aggressive.

Ironically, research reported in 2013 by Edward Kabay and other University of Maryland scientists indicates that having timber rattlers in the neighborhood reduces the danger of the great suburban bugaboo, Lyme disease. The rattlers are top forest predators that keep small rodents in check. Among them are mice that carry ticks responsible for Lyme disease. By studying the number of prey the snakes consume and the number of ticks on each animal, the research estimated that, for every timber rattlesnake at each study site, between twenty-five hundred and forty-five hundred ticks are eliminated from the environment annually.The timber rattlesnake is replaced in a north-south belt through the country's midsection by a relatively small—three feet maximum—shy rattler called the massasauga. It remains common in many areas, but in parts of the Midwest has been endangered by agriculture and developments. Thus, scientists were surprised in 2006 when a tiny pocket of them was found in a small area of Cook County, Illinois. Cook County is the county that includes Chicago.

The other U.S. pit viper, the cottonmouth—so-called because when it opens its mouth, the white interior is exposed—has a reputation for savage aggression. Not completely true, but some males are highly territorial, and cottonmouths of all sexes will coil up and stand their ground when threatened. Cottonmouths have potentially lethal venom. Superb swimmers, they are semiaquatic, eating fish and salamanders as well as small mammals. When need be, they are proficient hunters ashore. Cottonmouths inhabit the southeastern quadrant of the country, exclusive of Appalachia, and extend up the Mississippi River drainage to extreme southern Illinois and Indiana. Texas marks their western boundary. Particularly in the southern part of their range, where there is water there probably are cottonmouths.

Nowhere is this more true than in Louisiana, where cottonmouths account for the majority of snakebites. Not only are the snakes abundant, but the large number of Louisianans who live in and around swamps and bayous, and the significant number of these who are outdoor recreationists, fosters contact.

The cottonmouth's close but much less dangerous relative, the copperhead, inhabits a similar range but is absent from peninsular Florida, and edges north into the Ohio River valley, the Middle Atlantic states, the prairie states, and southern New England.

Although when finally aroused, copperheads can strike swiftly, they are generally docile, lethargic, and unobtrusive, blending well with fallen leaves. Because they stay out of the way, they are more likely to survive in settled areas from which other venomous snakes have been driven. They are especially fond of dry, rocky hillsides. Such was the exact habitat on which a wealthy New Yorker chose to erect his country manor in a town near mine. I was taken there by a friend, a well-known area herpetologist who had removed and translocated some of the snakes at the request of the owner. The home provided a beautiful view of the countryside, perched as it was atop a rocky cliff, but its doorway was literally a few feet away from perfect copperhead denning sites, meaning that the problem was something the master of the castle would have to deal with ad infinitum.

Their small size—a large copperhead is generally three feet long or so—enables them to creep into and hide in dwellings. Case in point: a man in Olanthe, Kansas, was in his dark but fully finished basement when what he thought was a wasp stung him on the foot. When he switched on the light, he saw a copperhead, which experts said might have been seeking shelter from the heat. The man was treated with a course of antivenom.

The severity—or lack thereof—of a copperhead bite can be gauged by a study of ninety-seven cases early in the twentieth century, when snakebite treatment was not as refined as it is today. Only five were fatal, two of which were youngsters, aged six and nine years. The other victims, all males, received no treatment except belts of whiskey, which in the early 1900s was still considered an effective antidote, even by experts, but actually speeds venom transfer by increasing blood flow.

In April 2002, a seven-year-old boy was bitten near some brush in his backyard by a copperhead in the suburb of Moon, Pennsylvania, eight miles from Pittsburgh International Airport and twelve miles from the heart of the city. One might not expect venomous snakes in a town of twenty-five thousand people, so close to a major city, not to mention one that has received awards for its quality of suburban life. Still, the boy was bitten on the leg, which swelled, requiring physicians to make incisions to relieve pressure. The boy was also treated with antivenom.

A man in my town was bitten twice by copperheads while working on a brush pile in his yard, which is near rocky ledges. The first time, he was slightly nipped on the shin. Because the only symptoms were a slight pain and redness, he did not seek medical attention. The second time, when both of the snake's fangs struck his hand, his arm swelled and hurt fiercely. He was treated at a hospital emergency room.

That venomous snakes might be neighbors is not something that many people think about when building their homes in New England. Indeed, venomous snakebites are relatively rare in the northern, densely populated states, although they do occur from time to time. For the present, at least, there is absolutely nothing to fear in Alaska, northern New England, or the extreme upper Midwest, where no venomous species live. It gets dicier in the western states, where rattlesnakes are abundant, and downright dangerous across the southern tier of the land, which has the highest density and diversity of venomous species. States such as Florida, Georgia, Louisiana, Arizona, and California rack up the highest number of bites and fatalities.

Within those states, even some of the largest metropolitan areas in the country have their complement of truly dangerous serpents. According to an online advisory on the venomous snakes found in and around Houston, produced by the Houston Zoo, western pygmy rattlers and copperheads inhabit the city. Cottonmouths are "abundant" in Houston and its vast environs, which covers more than ten thousand square miles, larger than New Jersey, and holds six million people. Houston proper, population two million plus, is six hundred square miles, big enough to hold the cities of Philadelphia, Baltimore, Chicago, and Detroit, as noted by National Public Radio. What keeps the place from becoming a traffic nightmare is that it holds many self-contained neighborhoods, where work is close to home for many people. Thus, it has been both castigated and praised as a prime example of urban sprawl. The flat landscape outlying Houston into which urbanization is advancing contains patches of wetlands and other open space, making it ideal habitat for species such as the cottonmouth. Moreoever, the region is laced with slow-moving bayous that serve as highways for snakes such as the cottonmouth.

Cottonmouth bites, according to the Houston Zoo, are "few" in the region, but encounters with people do occur. In 2011, a gardener killed a behemoth of a cottonmouth—five feet long—in a backyard in League City, a municipality of more than eighty thousand people in the greater Houston area.

The marshy, swampy terrain around Tampa, Florida, is prime cottonmouth habitat. This, combined with an explosive growth in human population, may be why cottonmouth scares have occurred there in recent years. With good reason. Within less than a year, in December 2007 and October 2008, cottonmouths struck two people in residential areas. The first victim was a boy, seven, who was running barefoot with friends across a backyard at a Sunday-afternoon birthday party. Innocent childhood fun brought him within range of a cottonmouth, which jabbed him in the foot. Although his condition was at first touch and go, the boy recovered after treatment. His parents vowed that neither he nor they would ever again venture outside barefoot.

The next victim was a former New Yorker, a forty-five-year-old mother who tried to protect a group of children from a cottonmouth outside the clubhouse of her gated community. Her intentions were good, but her mistake could have been lethal. She grabbed the snake to fling it away but it twisted its sinuous body and bit her on each hand. Her ordeal—during and after ten days in the hospital—was such that she was featured on Animal Planet.

In areas where cottonmouths are common, people must keep in mind the potential threat they pose. A teenage boy was walking home from school in Miramar, Florida, during February 2013, and saw a cottonmouth on the ground. Accidentally dropping something he was carrying near the snake, he bent over to retrieve it, thinking the snake was not within striking distance. It was, and bit the boy on the arm. He recovered.

The victims described above were lucky. In September 2008, a cottonmouth in the North Carolina piney woods killed a U.S. Army Special Forces trainee during land navigation training. Searchers found his lifeless body with multiple cottonmouth bites.

A year after the Tampa incidents, cottonmouths disturbed by highway construction near an expanse of wetlands swarmed over a neighborhood in Jacksonville, Florida. One homeowner was quoted in the news media as having killed ten of the snakes. Cottonmouths are a seemingly fearless snake and will enter buildings, including attached home garages. So discovered one woman in a Gainesville, Florida, subdivision in 2009 when she entered her garage to retrieve an item. Hiding under her son's toy automobile was a cottonmouth, which bit her on the toe. She recovered after three days in the hospital.

The ability of the cottonmouth to penetrate the most unlikely citadels of human habitation was proven in October 2010. A Rhode Island conventioneer was bitten on the leg as he walked along a path near a swimming pool at the upscale J. W. Marriott Grande Lakes resort near Orlando.

Many guests were upset by the incident, but not nearly as much as the management of the pricey getaway. A resort executive felt it necessary to deliver an elaborate statement to the press on its readiness to deal with threats from animals. The resort complex is bordered by a stream that is a wildlife haven and water source for the Everglades.

Once inside a dwelling, it is difficult to predict where a snake like a cottonmouth may lurk, even within the most private inner sanctum of a home. So discovered a Jacksonville, Florida, woman one night in July 2005 when she got up at night to use the toilet. What happened next is the stuff of nightmare. As she opened the lid on the john, a cottonmouth erupted from within it and bit her on the leg. The family later speculated the snake had entered through a dog door. Quick treatment enabled the victim to recover.

Venomous snakes do seem to strike from the most unlikely places in the urban/suburban landscape that people have created. About the same time frame (2007–2008) that an area in Tampa experienced two cottonmouth bites, an eastern diamondback holed up in a mailbox in a well-tended subdivision. When the mailman opened the door to remove a package, it bit him on the finger. The postman told reporters that he shook the snake off his digit by banging it against a car. If neither the elements nor gloom of night stays mailmen from their appointed rounds, neither, at least in the case of one of them, does a rattlesnake bite. Despite fiery pain in his arm, the mailman finished his route before seeking medical help.

If a recent trend continues, big-box stores, especially their garden centers, may gain the reputation as among the truly dangerous habitats for snakebite. Pit vipers have bitten people in more than one Wal-Mart in Florida, and others in Washington State, South Carolina, and Idaho. In 2010, a female employee at a Lowes Garden Center in Pensacola,

Florida, was struck by an eastern diamondback after, not re-alizing its species, she grabbed it by the tail to expel it from the store.

If a single strike from one snake is bad, multiple bites from several can be horrendous. It happens. It took twenty-four vials of antivenom to treat a California teenager after she stepped into a rattlesnake den in November 2012. She appeared to have been bitten by one adult and four young snakes. Sometimes the proverbial "den of vipers" is an ac-tual den of pit vipers. A thirteen-year-old Florida boy made headlines for his heroism in 2006 when, despite suffering four bites, he carried his ten-year-old friend on his back to prevent him from being bitten as well. The boy deposited his friend at a house several yards from where the bites—apparently from adult and baby rattlesnakes—occurred.

While children generally are perceptive enough to stay away from big snakes that appear dangerous, they are drawn to the highly toxic coral snake, with its bright colors and characteristic docility. Its coloration serves as a warning to the snake's enemies but attracts the human eye. Public health authorities say that one of the greatest dangers posed by this snake is that its visual appeal tempts young children to pick it up for play. Indeed, coral snakes can be so inoffensive that people have handled them without injury. A six-year-old boy in Naples, Florida, was not so lucky in 2012. He was used to the family's small ball python, kept as a pet, so was unafraid of snakes. When a coral snake came near while he was play-ing on the porch of his home, he reached for it and was bit-ten on the hand. The snake's docility, plus its small fangs and weak bite, accounts in part for the fact that only about twen-ty cases of coral-snake envenomation occur annually. Once bitten, however, a victim has a tough road ahead. A Miramar, Florida, man wearing sandals was struck as he walked out the door of his home in August 2012. His leg was seared by pain and ballooned, and his tongue went numb. Ten vials of antivenom were needed to treat him. The swelling persisted for weeks. The same amount of antivenom was needed to treat the six-year-old Naples boy. The envenomation was so severe, the boy flatlined twice at the hospital. Typical of bad coral-snake bites, the venom impaired his respiration; he had to be connected to a ventilator to keep breathing, enabling him to survive.

Not surprisingly, the time of year when most snakebites occur is from spring to fall, the exact months depending on the area of the country involved. During the winter, snakes retreat into underground and sheltered dens except in the warmest parts of the country. Weather and climate influence the timing and frequency of snakebite today, and the changing climate portends even more impact in the future. Floods in real snake country such as Louisiana send hordes of snakes toward high ground, where they encounter people who also are seeking safety. When Hurricane Katrina hit, scores of people reported brushes with venomous snakes, mostly cottonmouths. The danger from snakes during natural disasters is so real that the federal Centers for Disease Control (CDC) publishes a special fact sheet on the subject for both disaster workers and citizens. It warns people who have walked through water and found scratches on their body to check for snakebite.

Too little water as well as too much can up the number of snakebites. Drought in the Lake Havasu City area of Nevada in 2006 brought rattlesnakes near backyard pools, seeking both water and the small animals that are looking for a drink as well. Unusually hot, dry weather increases the chances of snakebite in two ways. Snakes wander farther in search of food. High daytime temperatures, which drive snakes into the cool underground in the wild, reducing chance encounters, also sends them looking for shelter in homes and other buildings, raising the odds. Snakes also avoid heat by staying up at night, so caution is merited after dark. An abundance of rain in arid areas can also increase the odds of being bitten by encouraging the growth of vegetative cover that helps young snakes survive.

Both rain-induced spurts in plant growth and long-term drought, as well as higher-than-usual temperatures can be linked to the way the incidence of snakebites has been trending upward and starting earlier since the beginning of the century. From California to Georgia, health authorities and hospital emergency rooms have been reporting surges in bites. Reports of spikes in bites have come from across the land, including Arizona, Utah, and Kansas, and Texas, Alabama, and Georgia. After unusually heavy monsoon rains in 2006, Arizona poison-control authorities attributed a hike in bites to a higher survival rate among young rattlesnakes due to more vegetative cover and water than usual. Newspaper headlines in California reported a "huge leap" in the number of rattlesnake bites during spring 2012, with bites reported to the state Poison Control Center up 48 percent from the previous year. Authorities said an erratic winter weather pattern—typical of what experts predict will accompany climate change—was responsible for the surge. A wetter than usual winter in 2011 helped snakes survive. A drier than usual winter in 2012 reduced prey, forcing snakes to travel farther for food and drink. Unusually rainy weather was also given as the reason for an abundance of rattlesnakes in southern California back in 2006. Authorities in Texas and Georgia, on the other hand, have blamed drought for the mounting snakebite cases in their states.

If weather events seesawing between downpour and drought are temporary aberrations, then serpent numbers associated with them may follow normal boom and bust cycles. If, as many scientists believe, this is the pattern for a future marked by long-term climate change, will snake populations increase progressively? Public health officials in snake country need to ponder the possibilities. It already may be happening. Early springs already have jump-started the snake season in several states, adding to the annual bite total. In 2012, according to *USA Today*, 129 snakebites were reported in California during April and May, compared to 70 the year before. Utah's total went from 3 to 8, Florida's were up 15 from the average of 220. Even before the summer of 2013 began, authorities in Texas were noting that snakes were abroad and biting people earlier than normal. If and when early spring becomes normal spring, will venomous snakes become more abundant than ever in historical times? And if warming allows pythons to expand north from South Florida, could coral snakes and eastern diamondbacks extend their range as far as the Northeast?

Another disturbing trend developed in California, where physicians and scientists have seen indications that the venom of certain rattlesnakes is becoming more toxic. In June 2012, a leading toxicologist and snakebite expert from the University of California at San Diego said the increase in venom potency may be a Darwinian case of only the strong survives. Richard Clark, MD, is director of the Division of Medical Toxicology at UC San Diego Health System and medical director of the California Poison Control System's San Diego Division. He noted that venom often changes toxicity with the seasons, weaker in winter and strong in summer, when snakes are actively hunting and staking out territory. At the same time, he addressed signs that something else is happening, that overall rattlesnake venom is packing an increasingly powerful jolt.

"We really don't know why the venom is becoming increasingly potent," he said in a statement issued by the university. "Some speculate that with the modern world encroaching on nature it could be survival of the fittest. Perhaps only the strongest, most venomous snakes survive."

In 2009, science writer Michael Tennesen interviewed several California snakebite experts who offered other explanations (ScientificAmerican.com, April 7, 2009). One possibility was that some rattlesnakes were evolving a more powerful weapon to deal with developing immunity to their venom. Another was that the array of rattlesnakes was changing, with the much more toxic Southern Pacific rattler replacing less adaptable species that had declined due to human activities.

The jury remains out on all the speculation. Consider, however, the evidence thus far: Venom is more toxic in summer. Snakes prosper during erratic weather patterns. Climate change is raising ambient temperatures, not exactly to endless summer but more of it. Climate change creates drastic swings in weather. Given all that, the impact on snakes and snakebite is not difficult to figure.

A study in 2013 by University of Illinois researcher Patrick Weatherhead suggests that global warming may benefit rat snakes—that's "rat," as in the snake I took on the airplane, not "rattle," as my fellow passengers heard. Hotter days might promote greater activity after dark, thus shielding these snakes from predators such as hawks, according to a description of the study released by the university on January 8, 2013. As a result, rat snake numbers might increase. Who is to say the same won't occur with respect to venomous snakes?

Safety Tips: Venomous Snakes

Go to the Internet and you will find a plethora of advice on how to avoid snakebite and what to do if avoidance does not work. Many state health and wildlife agencies publish that sort of information. Advice from governmental agencies and recognized medical facilities and organizations is generally solid.

Most victims of snakes know they have been bitten. Occasionally, the bite may go unnoticed or not recognized as such, such as in the case of a young child who is in discomfort but cannot explain why, or someone who is wading and is unable to identify the source of a sharp pain in the foot. The symptoms of a bite vary according to the snake, the amount of venom, and the overall health and age of the victim. Generally, however, some of the following may occur.

- one or two puncture marks in the skin at the wound site
- redness, swelling, and burning pain at the wound
- nausea or vomiting
- increased salivation and sweating
- Fever or chills
- Weakness, sometimes fainting
- Numbness and tingling, especially in the limbs, face, and mouth
- generalized bleeding or hemorrhage

If you or someone accompanying you is bitten, the first move is to get away from the snake. It is important to identify the snake. If possible, snap a photo with a cell phone camera. Try to remember key traits of the snake, such as coloring and shape of head. The key to on-scene treatment before medical help arrives is to stay calm. If a child is the victim, reassure him or her that all will be well. Call 911 or other emergency help immediately. The victim should lie down and rest, with the wound positioned below the heart until help comes. If possible, wash the wound with soap and water. If possible, apply a clean dressing. Jewelry such as rings and tight clothing should be removed before swelling develops. Keep the victim warm to avoid shock. Note the time of the bite and inform emergency personnel.

Here is what not to do:

- Do not pick up the snake or try to catch it.
- Do not wait for symptoms to appear before calling for help.
- Do not apply a tourniquet.
- Do not slash the wound with a knife, as in making the traditional X.
- Do not suck out venom.
- Do not apply ice, which new research suggests worsens the damage.
- Do not drink alcohol; it will increase blood flow and facilitate the flow of venom through the body.
- Do not drink caffeinated beverages.

Of course, the best protection against snakebite is to avoid being bitten. Here are some precautions to take if outdoors in snake country:

- Be aware that rattlers do not always rattle before a defensive strike.
- On hikes, try and keep to the trail, and wear loose-fitting trousers and over-the-ankle boots. Some outdoorsy types like to hike in shorts and sandals. In real snake country, that is an invitation to the emergency room.
- Avoid thickets and tall grass where snakes may shelter during the heat of the day.
- Do not stick your hands into nooks and crannies if you cannot see what is inside. Step on, not over, rocks and fallen logs. Do not sit on a log or stop before checking it out.

Even if you are not out in the wild, if there is a likelihood that venomous snakes are in the area, children should know the above precautions. Children should be taught to respect snakes and to leave them alone. As my son, who was playing with a baby rattlesnake in my driveway, proved, children are curious and may try to pick up snakes. Especially in cottonmouth country, tell children to keep away from brush and tall grass near water unless with an adult. Cottonmouths will bite both atop the surface and under water. Many people have been bitten while reaching over the side of a boat to bring up a string of fish or while dangling their hands in the water. Rattlesnakes swim well, too, even reaching offshore barrier islands like those off the Georgia coast.

Especially if there are children in the household, you can manage your property to discourage encounters with venomous snakes. The University of Florida's Institute of Food and Agricultural Sciences has excellent advice on how to "snake proof" yards. The precautions suggested are reasonable, allowing a homeowner to keep dangerous snakes at a distance but not at the price of making the property ecologically sterile. Mowing tall grass and trimming vegetation near buildings is advised, but not to the edges of ponds or other water, where frogs and turtles may seek shelter. Brush piles shelter a variety of wildlife, including snakes, so while these are not advisable near the house or playing areas, some of them should be left if space allows. Remember that rock walls and piles of lumber and firewood may also provide hiding spots for snakes.

As noted in the previous chapter, snakes can squeeze through openings that may seem much too small to admit them, so gaps under doors, unscreened drain pipes, holes in walls, or openings under the eaves of a building invite their entrance, particularly if they need shelter from temperature extremes. Door sweeps, weather stripping, caulking, and hardware cloth work in sealing out snakes. Pet doors provide access for snakes as well as cats and dogs. Eliminating rats, mice, and other rodents has the side benefit of reducing prey that will attract snakes.

If you see a snake, keep calm. Please, resist the knee-jerk response to try and kill it. The snake wants nothing to do with you. The only good reason for killing a snake is if it is venomous and poses an immediate threat to someone. If the encounter is outdoors, keep children and pets away and, if you are able, try to identify it as either venomous or harmless. Do not stand between the snake and cover to which it might flee. If you think the snake is not venomous, the best course is to leave it alone, because it will probably leave. Spraying it with water from a hose will encourage it to do so. If it is venomous, you can call a professional animal-control service or the local authorities. If a venomous snake turns up inside your home, get away from it. Call authorities or a wildlife-removal specialist immediately.

There is no substitute for studying a few good field guides for learning snake identification. Here, however, are a few tips. Several harmless snakes engage in behavior that resembles or even mimics their venomous relatives. Racers, gopher snakes, and hognosed snakes coil up and hiss, looking as mean as the nastiest rattlesnake. Rattlesnakes are stouter, with the characteristic triangular head of the pit viper. Its eyes have elliptical, not round, pupils. Between the nostrils and eyes, heat-sensing pits may be visible. The trademark rattle, not fully developed in young, has been known to break off of adult tails.

Many a water snake have been killed by people who confuse them with cottonmouths. Indeed, as far north as New England, water snakes are called "moccasins." Not venomous, water snakes are feisty and do bite. I found that out as a boy when I tried to collect one from a brook. The bite stung, but the pain subsided in moments. One way to tell a water snake from a cottonmouth is by the shape of the head. Although water snakes tend to flatten it when disturbed, the head is rather slender compared to the heavy, diamond-shaped head of the cottonmouth, which also bears heat-sensing pits. The cottonmouth's body is heavy, much stouter than that of a water snake.

Coral snakes have three harmless mimics, the scarlet kingsnake, the scarlet snake, and the milk snake. These non-venomous snakes mask themselves as coral snakes to discourage predators. The coloration of the harmless species resembles the red, yellow, and black circular bands of the coral snake. There are many variations of an old saying that describes the key to distinguishing between the venomous coral snake and its mimics. Here is one version: "Red next to yellow kills a fellow. Red next to black won't hurt Jack." On the coral snake, each end of the red band is bordered by yellow, separating it from black. Red is bordered by black in the mimics. If in doubt, of course, wisdom dictates you leave the snake alone.

I am a student and teacher of martial arts. One of my teachers gave me a piece of advice I now give my students, about how to defend against a knife attack.

> *Do not get into a knife fight.*
> *Do not ever get into a knife fight.*
> *If you get into a knife fight, you are going to get cut.*

Rephrase this a bit and you've got the best advice I could offer about dealing with venomous snakes.

> *Do not mess with a venomous snake.*
> *Do not ever mess with a venomous snake.*
> *If you mess with a venomous snake, you are going to get bitten.*

CHAPTER 10

PEACEFUL COEXISTENCE:
Searching for a Balance

n 1988, when people were beginning to realize that Lyme disease was a legitimate plague looming over the suburban good life, I published an article in *Audubon* magazine describing the role of deer and ticks in its ecology. I described how in some suburbs, the threat of the disease had turned former deer lovers into deer haters. I focused on attitudes of people living along Argilla Road in Ipswich, Massachusetts, an elegant neighborhood of landed mansions and McMansions on the North Shore. The road leads to scenic Crane Beach, on the ocean and part of a vast wildlife preserve that was once the estate of an early-twentieth-century Chicago industrialist.

I noted then that the well-heeled residents of Argilla Road had something in common with poor farmers I had interviewed in Africa. They were as hostile to the deer that were swarming over Crane Beach and spilling onto private land as the African farmers were to elephants that trampled and consumed their maize. Both the Massachusetts gentry and the African agriculturalists viewed their animal neighbors as a menace meriting elimination, no mercy granted. One woman who lived in the Argilla neighborhood told me that she had once sympathized with animal rightists who wanted to protect deer. She had since changed her mind. "To coexist with deer has become a nightmare," she wrote to the magazine in response to an earlier article in *Audubon* on deer that led me to her.

The turmoil that surrounded the deer of Crane Beach heralded the influx of wildlife into people space that is becoming more and more problematic. Finding a balance between man and beast is more difficult than ever. Emotion is as important a part of the equation as intellect, pragmatism, and principle. Biologists charged with managing wildlife populations must take into account the attitudes of people toward wildlife as well as the realities of how wild creatures interact with their environments. In California, animal control officials are faced with the quandary of reducing cougar attacks on humans without the use of sport hunting as a management tool, because public opinion will not support it. On the other side of the country, in the New York City suburb of Rye, managers of two nature preserves where coyotes and deer found refuge took heat from residents alarmed by coyote attacks on people. Worried residents, for the most part denied the use of firearms for protection, armed themselves with golf clubs and baseball bats for defense against the marauding beasts.

Residents of the Argilla neighborhood, located in a town with some of the most restrictive hunting regulations in the state, had once loved and even fed the deer. In 1983, the Massachusetts Division of Fisheries and Wildlife advised the nonprofit organization responsible for Crane Beach that the deer population surpassed the carrying capacity of the habitat. The agency advised a controlled deer hunt to solve the problem. Many residents bleated in protest against decimation of their beloved deer. They changed their tune after 40 percent of people in the neighborhood contracted Lyme disease. Residents demanded that the state legislature bestow home-rule powers on the town fathers that would allow them to open a year-round deer season for Ipswich landowners.

In an interview with me, the same woman who had

written to *Audubon* about deer told me of her testimony before a state legislative committee, when she asked, "What could be more damaging to one's property . . . than to have all the pleasure of sitting on the front lawn and working in the garden taken from us? To worry about little children playing on the lawn? We do not want to share our lawns with deer any longer."

It should be noted that, where deer hunting is a part of life, no one complains about too many deer, even if Lyme disease is rampant. The risk of contracting Lyme disease is a price most deer hunters are willing to pay for a larder full of venison.

The state would not accede to local control, but eventually a regulated hunt was held on the preserve that reduced the deer population there from more than three hundred to near fifty. Deer density per square mile went from more than one hundred to less than ten, and the number of ticks reported in scientific surveys dropped by about half. Although it is not an absolute, research in several areas suggests that culling of deer breaks the life cycle of ticks and reduces or even eliminates the incidence of Lyme disease.

After deer were eliminated from Monhegan Island, off the coast of Maine, the tick population there dropped significantly, and so did the infection rate of Lyme disease. After controlled hunts reduced deer in the Mumford Cove community of Groton, Connecticut, incidence of Lyme among residents decreased by 83 percent.

Culling—read that "killing"—is the most drastic and obvious way of reducing populations of wildlife when the need arises. Short of using nukes, however, it does not work in all situations. Efforts by state and federal authorities to kill off the Burmese pythons in the Everglades and beyond have barely dented the population there. Since 1995, according to the Florida Museum of Natural History, less than two thousand of the snakes have been removed from a population that may number more than one hundred thousand individuals.

In January 2013, the Florida Fish and Wildlife Conservation Commission (FWC) kicked off its month-long "Python Challenge" with a $1,000 reward to the hunter who brought in the longest python. More than fifteen hundred hunters slogged into the field. The take was only sixty-eight snakes, not many, considering the overall population and the hoopla surrounding the event. Despite the low bag, the FWC touted the event as a success, maintaining in a January 12, 2013, press release that its primary goals were "to raise public awareness and increase the agency's knowledge base regarding this invasive species and how to better understand and address impacts on the Everglades ecosystem, including native wildlife."

The FWC decided to suspend the challenge for 2014, focusing instead on trained python hunters to remove Burmese pythons and other nonnative reptiles from state lands. As things now stand, the prospect of controlling the pythons by hunting seems about as easy as cutting off the Hydra's heads. Hunting does work, on the other hand, for creatures such as deer.

Animal-protectionist groups, as they are wont to do, have protested python hunts. They challenged claims that the pythons are decimating Everglades mammals, charging that disease or poor management are responsible for the mammalian decline. *Protectionists* is the term I use, perhaps too loosely, to cover groups that promote animal rights, protection of animals regardless of conservation status, and what some of them feel is animal welfare, even if it is not conservation-based. Their philosophy is pretty much to leave nature alone or, at its least extreme, to avoid hunting, culling, or other activities they deem cruel to animals. By and large, they are antiscience, or propound false science. I use the term to distinguish them from conservationists, who by definition of the word *conservation* promote "wise use" of wildlife and other natural resources. Wise use mandates management of natural resources based on science as well as adherence to rules and laws established toward achieving that end.

Modern wildlife management as a scientific discipline was pioneered by an Iowan, Aldo Leopold, who was a 1908 Yale University forestry graduate. The writings of Leopold, who was a director of the National Audubon Society, presaged the modern environmental movement and outlined the principles of wildlife ecology that are the foundation for wildlife-management science.

As Leopold's career began to peak, in 1937 Congress passed the Federal Aid in Wildlife Restoration Act, better known as the Pittman-Robertson Act, which kickstarted wildlife management by the states. Funds from taxes on sales of firearms and ammunition mandated under the act have provided more than $5 billion to states for wildlife conservation, including habitat preservation. Originally, the act and wildlife-management science focused on game species, which is why the wildlife agencies of some states are still known as fish and game departments. This nomenclature is changing as the focus shifts to promoting biological diversity rather than a few select game species.

Wildlife managers dealing with urban wildlife problems, such as helping people coexist with deer, tussle with social and economic issues as well as practice science. They must balance the needs of people who enjoy watching a bear waddle through the neighborhood with those who are scared stiff of the beast. Their job involves application of scientific principles—and sometimes gut instinct—to harmonize the needs of wildlife, people, and the overall environment. Wildlife management amounts to a balancing act that takes the needs of human and animal life into account so that both benefit. The journal *Science* may have said it best in the 2006 article "The Carnivore Comeback," mentioned earlier, about the comeback of large carnivores in Europe, which is also experiencing a wildlife renaissance. It quoted John Linnell of the Norwegian Institute for Nature Research, who said that, when it comes to smoothing relations between people and wild animals, "Understanding the sociology of coexistence is the key."

Earlier in this book we looked at the principle of biological carrying capacity, the sustainable number of a species that a given habitat can support. Wildlife biologists must deal as well with another aspect of carrying capacity, that associated with human attitudes. Sociocultural carrying capacity is the number of animals that people will tolerate around them, depending on factors such as safety and economics. To again use Africa as an example, a farmer in Zimbabwe might be unwilling to endure elephants in his neighborhood if they are eating up his livelihood. But he might tolerate at least some of them if he derives income from tourists and sports hunters who pay to watch or hunt elephants. A neighborhood in New England may have sufficient trees, brush, and herbs to provide food and cover for deer, and enough water for them to drink, but if residents are continually smashing into them with their cars at night, the deer will not be seen as a good fit.

The activities and attitudes of humans are part of the management equation. Human attitudes toward wildlife vary widely. The nymphs of People for the Ethical Treatment of Animals (PETA) who protest fur fashions by baring all have a vastly different view of wildlife than the crusty codgers at National Rifle Association headquarters in Virginia. Ironically, the two groups are bedfellows on one issue, as both have opposed the reintroduction by the U.S. Fish and Wildlife Service of wolves in the West. The NRA panders to ranchers who view wolves as stock killers, hunters who fear four-footed competition for elk, and states' righters who object to what they see as conservation force-fed by big government. PETA, for its part, opposes predator introduction as "unnatural."

Human attitudes therefore must be taken into account when it comes to managing wildlife, says Rick Jacobson, who heads up Connecticut's Wildlife Division. "We used science-based wildlife management always in the context of the social sciences," he told me. Attitudes of some animal lovers can be extreme. As an example, when a deer shot by a legal bow hunter dropped and died on her property in Redding, Connecticut, the protectionist landowner opted to let it rot before allowing the hunter to claim it.

Connecticut's most glamorous game species, the white-tailed deer, is a poster child for wildlife management in all its complexity. Deer management has more than one objective, explained Jacobson. Deer are managed as a renewable natural resource, owned by the public and harvested by hunters who consume their venison. Deer are managed as watchable wildlife, for enjoyment of the public. Economic factors figure into deer management as well. Biologists must maintain a balance between people and deer; they manage deer as a public benefit yet seek to reduce property losses, accidents, and health threats that the animals may cause.

When wildlife managers manipulate nature by culling individual animals to ensure populations stay balanced, they provoke the ire of animal protectionists, who detest such tinkering. "Nature balances animal populations," said Nancy Rice, spokesperson of the organization Friends of Animals, based in Darien, Connecticut, in a statement issued March 3, 2011, while opposing a hunt authorized by the wildlife bureau to thin deer starving on Charles Island in Long Island Sound. The stomachs of deer sampled were crammed with vegetation that provided bulk but minimal nutritional value.

"Nature takes care of its own" is a slogan of PETA, which demands a hands-off approach to wildlife. But even the everyday activities of humans, seemingly harmless, influence wildlife. "Each time you use electricity, you cause a turbine in a power plant to turn, which causes water to be drawn from a river, lake, or Long Island Sound, which causes a fish to be drawn into the turbine to die. In effect, you kill a fish every time you turn on a light," Jacobson says. Short of living one's life like the ascetic monk Simeon Stylites, atop a pole, even the most ardent protectionist cannot help but impacting nature just by existing in a modern society.

A curious meeting of minds by hunters and protectionists in opposition to a deer cull occurred on New York's Long Island in January 2014. Towns on Long Island's East End, including exclusive East Hampton, planned to initiate a U.S. Department of Agriculture–funded cull of three thousand deer by professional sharpshooters. Eastern Long Island is thick with deer and virtually without wild predators. Deer cause immense damage to crops and landscaping and have become a serious highway hazard. Animal lovers squawked at any killing; hunters opposed the cull because they wanted to do the job themselves.

Animal protectionists presuppose a lost Eden, a natural world in absolute balance that, if restored, would operate in perfect harmony without human intervention. Pristine nature is tough to find nowadays, as witnessed by the beer cans I have seen in the short grass of the Serengeti, the fast-food wrappers on peat islets in the Okefenokee, and soda bottles on the white sand floor of the Red Sea. The only wild tiger I have ever seen stalked through a forest in Thailand, wild enough, perhaps, but only a nine-iron shot from a public golf course. So much for nature in the raw. The "nature can do it" crowd ignores the fact that humans have been managing wildlife since prehistoric times. Think not? Pre-Columbian Americans systematically burned prairies to promote growth of grassland plants and maintain herds of prey such as deer and bison. Even when nature is pure, moreover, some animals may suffer. "An undisturbed ecosystem is not necessarily a stable one," noted Greg Yarrow, a professor of wildlife ecology at Clemson University, in a fact sheet on wildlife management available on the website of the Clemson Cooperative Extension.

The makeup of plant communities naturally changes—by succession, for example—creating a home for some animals one day, another group the next.

Besides a woeful lack of scientific literacy, another reason fueling the emotional antipathy of protectionists toward sound wildlife management is the anthropomorphism of nature that has been magnified by the mass media. It began with the rise of nature programming on television in the 1960s and 1970s, some of which was scientifically excellent but much of which made animals into people in furry suits. It took Peter Rabbit and the Big Bad Wolf to an entirely new level. I noted this trend in my book *Killer Animals*.

How could opposition to trapping for a living *not* mount after Henry Fonda, in the nature documentary *World of the Beaver*, aired nationally in 1970, intoned such anthropomorphic mush as what follows?

> *Castor [the beaver] has been thinking about finding himself a wife, but he's surprised when he finds out that his parents want him to leave the pond. . . . It doesn't take very long before Castor discovers a friend in need. It's his good luck that she's just about the most beautiful thing he's ever seen. Look at those sensitive eyes; and, of course, any girl wearing a fur coat is hard to resist. . . . It's love at first sight.*

While the narrative may be amusing, the idea of a beaver falling in love distorts our understanding of animal behavior and is incompatible with the reality of ecological balance. Animals mate, fight, kill, and play in ways instinctively directed by their evolution. If the repertoire of an animal's predatory behavior includes a response to creatures the size of a human, then a human may well become its dinner. A hungry lioness killing on the savanna is a different beast entirely from the loving Elsa portrayed in *Born Free*.

The benign face of Mother Nature was promulgated on a Christmas card issued many years ago by the Humane Society of the United States. Cats, a fox, and weasels, superpredators of rabbits, cozily cuddle up to two furry bunnies. In real-life nature, Mother would grow fangs. Getting these creatures together would trigger a red slaughter, first of the bunnies, then between the predators as they fought for the scraps.

Again, several years ago, two top conservationists, John Madson and Ed Kozicky, summed up the impact of television on attitudes toward wildlife management in a speech to a student chapter of the Wildlife Society at Louisiana State University: "Many viewers began to feel that wildlife animals live in harmony in enchanted forests, a vision of freedom, peace and beauty that was missing from their own lives. In their newfound love of wildlife—whether real or imagined— they could not bear the thought of those wild creatures being hunted or trapped."

The situation has not changed. How else can you explain residents of Greenwood Village, a high-priced suburb of Denver, who in 2009 feuded with a hunter hired by the city to get rid of aggressive coyotes? Or the residents of a senior community in Oceanside, California, who howled because the board of directors decided to trap coyotes who were terrorizing their own neighbors in 2004? Or the whining of protectionists in 2009 when authorities killed eight coyotes in Griffith Park, Los Angeles, after coyotes sank their teeth into two people there? Or the residents and mayor of Glendale, California, who, inspired by animal protectionists, asked Los Angeles County to forgo killing a family of coyotes inhabiting a burned-out house? It is a solid bet that if coyotes killed or injured someone in any of these communities, attitudes would quickly change, just as Argilla Road residents shifted their views on deer.

Discourse and debate in communities where deer control is an issue reflect the complexities faced by officials who must deal with it as well as the spectrum of public opinion on the subject. Traditionally, debate waxes hottest in suburbs that are affluent and close to large urban centers. Seventeen miles from Boston, upscale Medfield, Massachusetts, has allowed bow hunting of deer since 2011. Among the residents supporting the hunt was an epidemiologist from the Cummmings School of Veterinary Medicine at Tufts University, who studies Lyme ticks. He opined, as quoted by the local press in November 2011, that hunting was the best way to reduce deer numbers—and ticks—to acceptable levels. A representative of PETA charged that deer were a "scapegoat."

At a town meeting in May 2013, residents of another Boston suburb, Weston, defeated a fierce campaign by the anti-hunting Weston Deer Friends to stop bow hunting of deer. An exclusive community, which has the highest per capita income in the state, Weston allowed a handful of bow hunters, screened and approved by the town, to take aim at deer from tree stands. The restrictive nature of the hunt did not satisfy animal protectionists, who campaigned for alternative methods: birth control, spraying deer with water, and landscaping with plants that deer find unpalatable.

Hastings-on-Hudson is an unashamedly progressive village in Westchester County, New York, a couple of minutes' ride north of the Bronx. It is a "Portlandia" east that the *New*

York Times, in a February 15, 2013, story, described as part of a burgeoning "hipsturbia" because of the attraction it holds for hip young professionals. When the town administrator suggested professional killing of swarming deer by netting and stunning them, residents, as reported in the Times, likened him to Hitler. The village decided to recruit volunteers who would put out potted plants that are the favored munchies of deer to help determine their numbers. Meanwhile, professionals would capture deer so that they could be injected with contraceptives every two years. More than one hundred deer inhabit the village's two square miles. Even if the deer in that scrap of landscape were rendered fawnless, short of erecting a dome over the whole village, nothing would prevent deer from surrounding towns from adding to the population.

Westport, Connecticut, a major commuter stop on the railroad to Grand Central Terminal, is another New York City suburb that disavows hunting. The home of real-life Mad Men and a place where no one raises eyebrows when a famous film face walks into the hardware store, it is the only town in the state to have an exemption from state law allowing it to ban hunting. Not surprising, then, that it has wrestled with a deer problem for years. The minutes of its so-called Deer Management Committee in January 2013 noted that any attempt to use professional sharpshooters would depend "on political and homeowner support" and that there was no support for reconsideration of its hunting ban. Westport is the site of a citadel of elegant equestrianism, the Fairfield County Hunt Club. The club got its name from fox hunts, in the traditional British manner, staged by a band of upper-crust residents of the town in the 1920s. Needless to say, foxes are safe in town nowadays.

Pittman-Robertson Act funds footed most of the bill for a massive study on managing urban deer in Connecticut, published in 2007 by the state's Department of Environmental Protection, now Energy and Environmental Protection. The study examined several options for deer control. Birth control, promoted by animal rights groups, is expensive, impractical, and just plain does not work. Sharpshooting is also expensive, up to $650 per deer, but can be used to reduce small populations in a given area. Deer, however, have a way of filling a vacuum and soon occupy vacant space. "Regulated hunting has proven to be an effective deer population management tool," according to the study. "It has been shown to be the most efficient and least expensive technique for removing deer and maintaining deer at desired levels."

Animal rights groups advocate the use of darting to inject does with birth control drugs, which according to biologists costs $1,000 per animal and is only a temporary fix, if that. Suffice to say that injecting deer has been tried only on captive and closed populations and has not worked on free-ranging deer. Moreover, up to 90 percent of does must be injected for even a chance of success.

Among conservation organizations, the Nature Conser-vancy has sterling credentials. Here is what that group has to say about contraception as a means of controlling deer, as part of why it allows deer hunting to maintain ecological harmony on some of its preserves in New York State. The remarks are included in a position paper on the organization's website.

While some groups may advocate contraceptive control measures, this approach has several drawbacks: Contraceptive control measures are currently commer-cially unavailable, and field testing has provided mixed results with high costs (estimates of $1,000 per deer were reported by the Northeast Deer Technical Committee 2008). While the use of contraceptives has proved effective on captive deer, none have *yet proved effective in controlling populations of wild, free-ranging deer (Bishop et al. 2007).*

As stated by DeNicola et al. (2000): "Unfortunately, much confusion surrounds the status of fertility control agents. The lack of public understanding regarding the availability and practicality of fertility control has caused unnecessary delays in the implementation of effective management programs, because fertility control is perceived as the ideal solution. To put fertility control technology in perspective, after four decades of research, effective anti-fertility programs for controlling populations of free-ranging wildlife simply do not exist."

This conclusion was also verified by Audubon Pennsylvania (Latham et al. 2005). Furthermore, no fertility control agents have been federally approved for the management of wildlife populations in the United States, and application of fertility control to wildlife can only occur within a research context (Jeremy Hurst, NYS DEC State Deer Biologist, pers. comm.). Four such research studies have occurred within New York. More research is needed with contraception before this can be depended upon for cost effective control; TNC preserves may offer an ideal setting for future contraception testing. At this time though, contraception is not a feasible option.

About birth control for Bambi, enough said.

I should note that while I am a hunter, I have no desire to hunt predators. I take grim satisfaction in viewing them as kin. At the same time, I am in favor of sport hunting of any species if sound management principles dictate.

Black bears, like deer, are cuddly, affable animals in the eyes of many animal lovers, which is why hunts for this thriving species in states unaccustomed to bagging bruins bring out the protesters en masse. New Jersey has scheduled hunts every year or two since 2003.

The bear hunt has been a legal tug-of-war between animal rights groups and pro-hunting groups over the last decade. Hunts usually whittle down the state's bear population, which averages around three thousand animals, by a few hundred, keeping it manageable. The hunt is focused on the northern and northwestern parts of the state, the reservoir from which bears have trickled into virtually every corner of New Jersey.

Activists have used multiple weapons, from lawsuits to illegal demonstrations, to stop the hunts, some years successfully. One psychology professor shows up regularly to protest, carrying signs with plaintive messages like MOTHER NATURE IS CRYING.

Animal protectionists are crying as well in states that increasingly are stiffening their defense against antimanagement forces. Oregon and Washington have ignored the screeches from animal protectionists and resumed legal hunting of cougars using hound dogs. The rationale is that cougar numbers need to be controlled to decrease the odds of attacks and livestock damage. Cougar hunting, however, is no easy proposition. The cats are so smart, it takes dogs trained to track and tree them for hunters to have any measure of success in the hunt.

Biologist Michelle LaRue, coauthor of the study that confirmed cougars were returning to the Midwest, was talking about that species when she said in a prepared statement, "The question is how the public will respond after living without large carnivores for a century."

California, where protectionists and the anti-hunting lobby exert great influence over wildlife-management policies—and where cougar attacks are a real concern—is bucking the tide. In spring 2013, the state Department of Fish and

Wildlife (CDFW) weakened the process under which special permits are issued to kill cougars that threaten people and livestock. It stipulated one cougar kill per permit, even if the individuals handling the problem are state wildlife officers. Encouraged by the department's retreat, protectionists pushed state lawmakers to further emasculate problem-cougar policy by passing legislation banning lethal action against problem cougars except in cases of "imminent threat to public health or safety." It went into effect in November 2013. In the bill's legalese, "imminent threat" is described as "a situation where a mountain lion exhibits one or more aggressive behaviors directed toward a person that is not reasonably believed to be due to the presence of responders." It is a far cry from Stand Your Ground. Among the suggested alternatives to lethal action are hazing the animal until it departs and "providing veterinary care." Protectionists used the killing of two young cougars under the porch of a home as a rallying point to push for the weak-kneed approach.

California seems to be doing all it can to create conditions favorable for another rash of attacks reminiscent of those in Cuyamaca Rancho State Park. The interests of both cougars and Californians of the human persuasion might be better served by a lesson from Louisiana and its alligators. The Internet Center for Wildlife Damage Management (ICWDM. org), affiliated with major universities, notes that "the historically low [alligator] attack rate in Louisiana is attributed to a history of intense hunting." Establishment of programs elsewhere is also having results, according to the center, which noted that "hunting pressure appears to be the most effective means of increasing alligator wariness and may be responsible for limiting the incidence of alligator attacks in Florida."

The power that protectionists wield in California was obvious in 2012 when the president of the California Fish and

Game Commission, Daniel W. Richards, was canned because he killed a cougar on a legal hunt in Idaho. The commission, of five members appointed by the governor and confirmed by the state, sets conservation policies such as hunting seasons, bag limits, and listing of endangered species. Richards's downfall came after a photograph of him with his trophy was posted on the Internet. Bear in mind, he did nothing illegal, but simply offended the protectionist sensibilities of too many Californians.

More than a dozen states, including Arizona, Washington, Utah, and the Dakotas, allow cougar hunting. Hunting does, of course, cut down on cougar numbers, so in that way might be viewed as a control factor. Given the small number of animals subtracted from the population, however, the impact is minimal. Exposure to hunters could make cougars more wary, but on the other hand, hunting might create stress that contributes to errant behavior by the cats, making them even nastier when they encounter humans. In summation, there is no proof that killing cougars stops them from killing us, except in the case of individual cats that have already killed and are likely to be repeat offenders.

Sport hunting is part of the cougar-management plans of the states that allow it. States with long-standing cougar populations gradually shifted from classifying the species as vermin to a game animal during the last decades of the twentieth century. States where animal rights sentiment is strong—California being the best example—fully protect cougars. Some states compensate owners if cougars take their livestock. Others have legal mechanisms by which aggrieved farmers and ranchers can take out the offending cougars on their own.

The contrast in approach states take to managing cougars often parallels the political divisions of red and blue, between Berkeley and Boise, if you will. Indeed, the politics and social mores of a state's human population often helps shape management of iconic species such as the cougar, and not always for the better. The difference in approach is exemplified by comparison of policies in Idaho, with a human population of 1.5 million, and California, with 35 million people. It was examined by Terry M. Mansfield of the Idaho Department of Fish and Game at the Seventy-Second North American Wildlife and Natural Resources Conference in 2007.

Both states want to maintain healthy cougar populations. California emphasizes protecting habitat, quick government response to public safety problems, and public education about cougars and their role in nature. Idaho focuses on managing cougars in conjunction with deer, elk, and other prey species so as to provide diverse hunting opportunities. For California wildlife managers, under mandated policy, cougars are valuable as iconic symbols of the wilderness. For those in Idaho, cougars may be magnificent creatures, but they also exist for sport hunting and the income it engenders.

The scientists who produced evidence of cougars spreading to the Midwest have emphasized the need for states there to have plans in place for enabling cougar-human coexistence. "We believe public awareness campaigns and conservation strategies are required across these states, such as the mountain lion response plans already in place in Nebraska and Missouri," said coauthor Michele LaRue in a statement released in 2012 by the University of Minnesota, where she was pursuing her doctorate.

Following the policy of states farther west, Nebraska and Missouri established plans for dealing with cougars once evidence supported their presence within state borders. The plans specify how wildlife officials and law enforcement should deal with cougar incidents, with guidelines for different types of events and how to handle problem lions. In some states, a cougar that appears to stalk people must be removed from the wild within twenty-four hours. Some plans even specify how to handle sightings of cougars. Plans for responding to a cougar incident even exist at a municipal level in some states with large cougar populations. An outcry by animal-protectionist groups forced the Santa Monica, California, police to modify their way of dealing with cougars after cops and state wildlife agents shot the young male that had penetrated the downtown district and caused a commotion in 2012.

All sorts of alternatives to destroying problem cougars are suggested by the California policy. Indeed, they all merit consideration for cougars and other urban wildlife but should be viewed realistically. Trapping and relocating problem animals sometimes solves problems, but more often than not, transported animals return. If not, they may trigger territorial battles in their new homes with members of their own species. Lacing garbage with noxious potions gives bears a belly ache but is unproven as a permanent discouragement, as is shooting them with rubber slugs. A better weapon is public education aimed at stopping practices such as feeding that attract wild animals and reduces their wariness of humans. If people know what to do and what not to do, and what to fear and what not to fear, conflicts with wild beasts lessen. Often, problems are best solved when wildlife managers can use multiple tactics.

Dealing with problem wildlife can be difficult and unpleasant. But it is better than the alternative, which almost always ends up in blanket attempts to eliminate the problem species rather than those individuals that make trouble. This applies especially to large, potentially dangerous creatures. People will tolerate a raccoon raiding garbage more than a bear, simply because the bear poses potential risk to life and limb. Carrying this point further, people may tolerate a bear that upends trashcans but definitely not one that attacks a child. Understandably, nothing arouses public sentiment against wild animals more than perceived threats to children.

The aim of conservationists and wildlife managers is to strike a balance between the new wildlife of suburbs and cities and the people who live there. It mandates not only control of problems but proactive planning to create environments supportive of both. Firstly, however, large species of animals such as bears and cougars need substantial expanses of wildland—strongholds and reservoirs—in order to maintain base populations. No amount of suburban greenery can substitute for big country. Beyond that, conservation planners in urbanizing areas need to make environmental corridors a keystone of open-space design.

The U.S. Department of Agriculture Natural Resources Conservation Service is at the forefront of corridor conservation. It advises that the best corridors are continuous, not fragmented. That wide corridors are better than narrow. That corridors should link other important natural features, and that the more ecologically and geologically diverse a corridor, the more useful it is.

Ultimately, whether or not the suburbs and cities, or anywhere, for that matter, will support a rich mix of people and wildlife will depend on our values, and the level of risk we are prepared to accept. Would it matter to us if we lived in a world where no cougars prowled? Would wood and field be robbed of their magic, be just so much vegetation, if deer did not haunt glade and cove? Do we wish to live in a world where nature exists only in sanitized and safe forms, like parks and preserves? It is easier, perhaps, to share the earth with potentially dangerous animals that run free only in faroff wild places. The crunch comes when we must decide whether or not we can accept them in our midst. Our ability to work out a balance with the other creatures that inhabit this planet may very well measure whether or not we have indeed evolved as a sapient species.

BIBLIOGRAPHY

Barker, David G., and Tracy M. Barker. "The Distribution of the Burmese Python, *Python molurus bivittatus.*" *Bulletin of the Chicago Herpetological Society* 43, no. 3 (2008): 33–38.

Beckmann, Jon P., and Carl W. Lackey. "Carnivores, Urban Landscapes, and Longitudinal Studies: A Case History of Black Bears." *Human–Wildlife Conflicts* 2, no. 2 (Fall 2008).

Beier, Paul. "Cougar Attacks on Humans in the United States and Canada." *Wildlife Society Bulletin* 19 (1991): 403–12.

Benson, John F., and Brent R. Patterson. "Moose *(Alces alces)* Predation by Eastern Coyotes *(Canis latrans)* and Eastern Coyote x Eastern Wolf *(Canis latrans x Canis lycaon)* hybrids." *Canadian Journal of Zoology* 91, no. 11 (2013): 837–41.

Berger, Kim M., and Eric M. Gese. "Does Interference Competition with Wolves Limit the Distribution and Abundance of Coyotes?" *Journal of Animal Ecology* 76, no. 6 (2007): 1075–85.

Bozarth, Christine A., et al. "Coyote Colonization of Northern Virginia and Admixture with Great Lakes Wolves." *Journal of Mammalogy* 92, no. 5 (2011): 1070–80.

Chambers, Steven M., et al. "An Account of the Taxonomy of North American Wolves from Morphological and Genetic Analyses." *North American Fauna* 77 (October 2012): 1–67.

Connecticut Department of Environmental Protection, Bureau of Natural Resources, Wildlife Division. *Managing*

Urban Deer in Connecticut: A Guide for Residents and Communities. 2nd ed. Hartford, CT: Bureau of Natural Resources, Department of Environmental Protection, 2007. www.ct.gov/deep/lib/deep/wildlife/pdf_files /game/urbandeer07.pdf.

Coss, Richard G., and E. Lee Fitzhugh et al. "The Effects of Age, Group Composition, and Behavior on the Likelihood of Being Injured by Attacking Pumas." *Anthrozoos: A Multiplinary Journal of the Interactions of People & Animals* 22, no. 1 (2009).

Culver, Melanie, et al. "Genomic Ancestry of the American Puma *(Puma concolor)*." *Journal of Heredity* 91, no. 3 (2000): 186–97.

Dorcas, Michael E., et al. "Severe Mammal Declines Coincide with Proliferation of Invasive Burmese Pythons in Everglades National Park." *Proceedings of the National Academy of Sciences* 109, no. 7 (2012): 2418–22.

Dorcas, Michael E., John D. Willson, and J. Whitfield Gibbons. "Can Invasive Burmese Pythons Inhabit Temperate Regions of the Southeastern United States?" *Biological Invasions* 13 (2011): 793–802.

Drummond, Mark A., and Thomas R. Loveland. "Land-Use Pressure and a Transition to Forest-Cover Loss in the Eastern United States." *BioScience* 60, no. 4 (2010), 286–98.

Enserink, Martin, and Gretchen Vogel. "The Carnivore Comeback," *Science* 314 (November 2006), 746–49.

Erickson, Gregory M., et al. "The Ontogeny of Bite-Force Performance in American Alligator *(Alligator mississippiensis)*." *Journal of Zoology* 260, no. 3 (2003): 317–27.

Fitzhugh, E. Lee, and David P. Fjelline. "Puma Behaviors During Encounters with Humans and Appropriate Human Responses." in *Proceedings of the 5th Mountain*

Lion Workshop, February 27–March 1, 1996, San Diego, CA. http://users.frii.com/mytymyk/lions/pumadfn.htm.

Gehrt, Stanley D., et al. "Population Ecology of Free-Roaming Cats and Interference Competition by Coyotes in Urban Parks." *PLoS One* 8, no. 9 (2013).

Gehrt, Stanley D., Seth P. D. Riley, and Brian L. Cypher, eds. *Urban Carnivores: Ecology, Conflict, and Conservation.* Baltimore: Johns Hopkins University Press, 2010.

Harvey, Rebecca G., et al. "Burmese Pythons in South Florida: Scientific Support for Invasive Species Management." University of Florida IFAS Extension, publication #WEC242. http://edis.ifas.ufl.edu/uw286.

Hermensen-Baez, L. Annie, Jennifer Seitz, and Martha C. Monroe. "Wildland-Urban Interface: Varied Definitions." University of Florida IFAS Extension, publication #FOR225. http://edis.ifas.ufl.edu/fr287.

Herrero, Stephen, et al. "Fatal Attacks by American Black Bear on People: 1900–2009." *Journal of Wildlife Management* 75, no. 3 (2011): 596–603.

Hoffman, Justin D., Hugh H. Genoways, and Jerry R. Choate. "Long-Distance Dispersal and Population Trends of Moose in the United States." *Alces* 42 (January 2006): 115–31.

Hristienko, Hank, and John E. McDonald Jr. "Going into the 21st Century: A Perspective on Trends and Controversies in the Management of the American Black Bear." *Ursus* 18, no. 1 (2007): 72–88.

Hubbard, Ryan D., and Clayton K. Nielsen. "White-Tailed Deer Attacking Humans During the Fawning Season: A Unique Human–Wildlife Conflict on a University Campus." *Human–Wildlife Conflicts* 3, no. 1 (2009): 129–35.

Kabay, Edward, Nicolas Caruso, and Karen Lips. "Timber Rattlesnakes May Reduce Incidence of Lyme Disease in the Northeastern United States." Paper presented at the annual meeting of the Ecological Society of America, Minneapolis, MN, August 6, 2013.

Kays, Roland, Abigail Curtis, and Jeremy J. Kirchman. "Rapid Adaptive Evolution of Northeastern Coyotes via Hybridization with Wolves." *Biology Letters* 6 (2009): 89–93.

Kyle, Christopher J. "The Conspecific Nature of Eastern and Red Wolves: Conservation Management Implications." *Conservation Genetics* 9, no. 3 (June 2008): 699–701.

Lackey, Carl W., Jon P. Beckmann, and James Sedinger. "Bear Historical Ranges Revisited: Documenting the Increase of a Once-Extirpated Population in Nevada." *Journal of Wildlife Management* 77, no. 4 (2013): 812–20.

Langley, Ricky L. "Alligator Attacks on Humans in the United States." *Wilderness & Environmental Medicine* 16, no. 3 (2005): 119–24.

LaRue, Michelle A., and Clayton K. Nielsen et al. "Cougars Are Recolonizing the Midwest: Analysis of Cougar Confirmations During 1990–2008." *Journal of Wildlife Management* 76, no. 7 (2012): 1364–69.

Meachen, Julie A., and Joshua X. Samuels. "Evolution in Coyotes *(Canis latrans)* in Response to the Megafaunal Extinctions." *Proceedings of the National Academy of Sciences* 109, no. 11 (2012): 4191–96.

Northeast Deer Technical Committee. *An Evaluation of Deer Management Options.* Bethesda, MD: Wildlife Society: May 2009.

Noyes, John H., and Ronald R. Progulske, eds. *A Symposium on Wildlife in an Urbanizing Environment, November 27–29, 1973, Springfield, Massachusetts.* Amherst: Cooperative Extension Service, University of Massachusetts, 1974.

Patterson, J. H. *The Man-Eaters of Tsavo and Other African Adventures.* New York: Macmillan, 1927.

Ricciuti, Edward R. *Killer Animals: The Menace of Animals in the World of Man.* New York, Walker, 1976.

———. *The New York City Wildlife Guide: Wild Creatures of New York and Where to Find Them.* New York: Schocken, 1984.

Servheen, Chris. Keynote address, Fourth International Human-Bear Conflict Workshop, March 20–22, 2012, Missoula, Montana. Summary: www.cfc.umt .edu/humanbearconflicts/Pdf/4th%20Human-Bear%20 Conflict%20Workshop%20Summary.pdf.

Spotte, Stephen. *Societies of Wolves and Free-Ranging Dogs.* New York: Cambridge University Press, 2012.

Von Holt, Bridgett N., et al. "A Genome-Wide Perspective on the Evolutionary History of Enigmatic Wolf-Like Canids." *Genome Research* 21, no. 8 (2011): 1294–1305.

Way, Jonathan G., et al. "Genetic Characterization of Eastern 'Coyotes' in Eastern Massachusetts," *Northeastern Naturalist* 17, no. 2 (2010), 189–204.

Wilson, Paul J., et al. "DNA Profiles of the Eastern Canadian Wolf and the Red Wolf Provide Evidence for a Common Evolutionary History Independent of the Gray Wolf." *Canadian Journal of Zoology* 78, no. 12 (2000): 2156–66.

Woodward, Allan R., and Dennis N. David. "Alligators." 2005. Internet Center for Wildlife Damage Management. www.icwdm.org/handbook/reptiles/Alligators.asp.

INDEX